CW01483767

GUNS N' ROSES

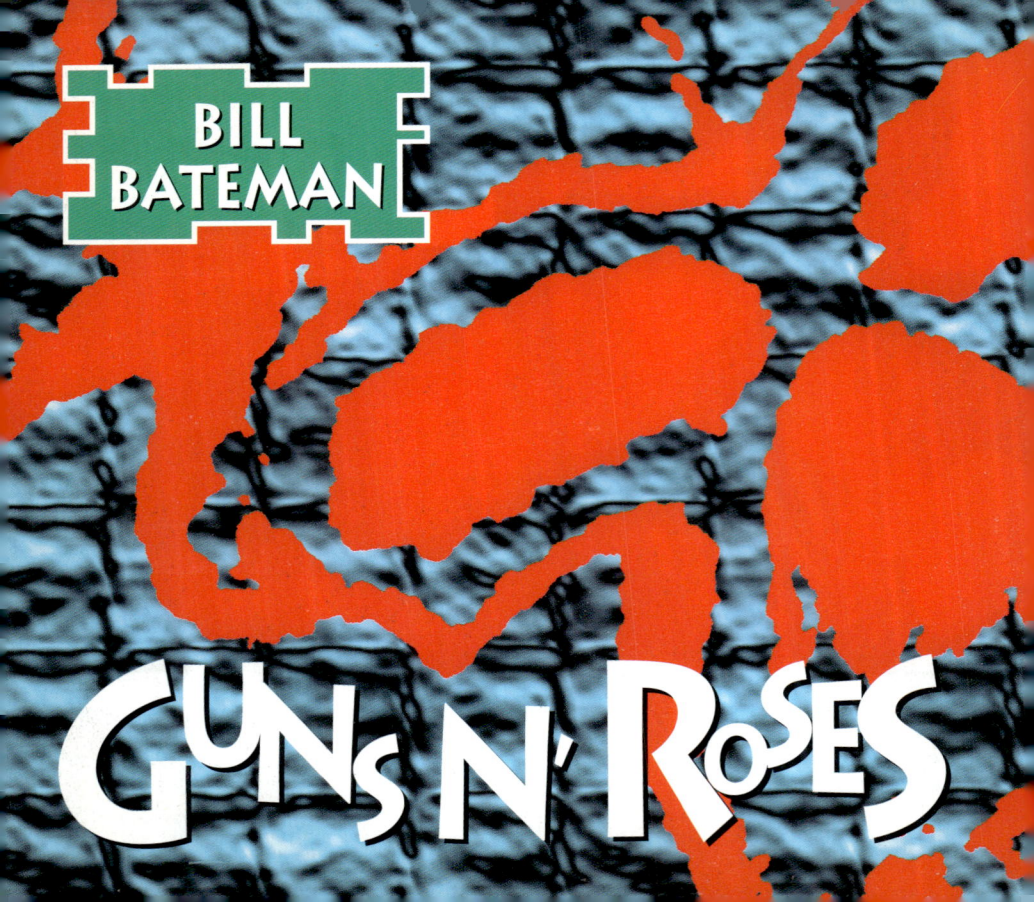

AN ORION PAPERBACK

This is a Carlton Book

First published in Great Britain in 1994 by Orion Books Ltd, Orion House,
5 Upper St Martin's Lane, London, WC2H 9EA.

Text and design © 1994 Carlton Books Ltd
CD Guide format © 1994 Carlton Books Ltd

A CIP catalogue record for this book is available from the British Library.

ISBN 1 85797 586 3

Edited, designed and typeset by Archetype Ltd.
Printed in Italy

THE AUTHOR

Bill Bateman is a rock journalist whose previous books include the story of Bon Jovi. His hobbies
range from raising snakes to riding unicycles. He first decided to write about Guns N' Roses when he
heard their unique version of 'Knocking On Heaven's Door'.

CONTENTS

GUNS N' ROSES
OF MYTHS AND MEN...

Monday, April 20, 1992. The end of the Easter weekend. For the religious, a time to contemplate the symbolism of a man rising from the dead to transcend mortality. For a roll call of rock and pop dignitaries, a time to celebrate the life of the late Freddie Mercury, super-group Queen's singer and figurehead, who'd succumbed to AIDS. For Guns N' Roses, a time for rebirth....

They'd operated as if under siege in recent years but it was now time to drop their warlike stance and rub shoulders with the great and the good in a common cause; to choose the positive instead of the negative. It was the day that, if only for an hour or two, Guns N' Roses finally grew up.

As 1991 moved into 1992, the band had blazed a trail across America and Europe bringing mayhem, media thunderstorms and, above all, their own malevolent bad attitudes. They couldn't keep any kind of deadline. Unable to release a record on time, they finally delivered two mammoth musical banquets: *Use Your Illusion Volumes I & II* . They'd leave concert crowds waiting late into the night and then jam into

Axl and Elton, united at the Freddie Mercury tribute concert

Slash and Brian May trading guitar licks at Wembley

the early hours, ignoring all curfews. They were unable to agree on things, even amongst themselves—ultimately demonstrated by the decision of founder-member Izzy Stradlin to leave. Incapable of dealing with the prying eyes of the media, they tried shutting them out—only to find themselves making more headlines than ever. At every turn, Guns N'

W Axl Rose, singer

The Wembley finale—Duff and Axl rub shoulders with Roger Daltrey of the Who.

Roses seemed to drive the wrong way up a one way street. Some days they thrived on the chaos; on others it sapped their strength, obliterating any sense of purpose. Their very existence seemed to go against the laws of nature.

But at Wembley Stadium on that Easter Monday, W Axl Rose—the man whose initials spell war—seemed a little less aggressive. If he wasn't quite asking for peace and forgiveness, it certainly looked as if he wanted a little understanding from the world.

Guns N' Roses' appearance at the Freddie Mercury Tribute Concert for AIDS Awareness did not pass without comment. Here was the band who'd sung about "faggots [who'd] spread some fucking disease" being asked to celebrate the life of one of rock's most flamboyant homosexuals. The irony was not lost on gay protest group *Act Up*, who made threats to disrupt Guns N' Roses' performance. But Brian May, Queen's legendary guitarist, reasoned that it was their lousy record on human rights that made the band an even more appropriate choice for the concert. This wouldn't be the usual hand-wringing tribute from a bunch of well-meaning liberals. This

would be the 'most dangerous band in the world' giving their fans an unambiguous warning about one of the most dangerous diseases of all time.

"If we succeeded in putting on a concert with people who are not normally associated with these things… and particularly if we can pull in someone like Guns N' Roses, who are normally thought to be the macho end of the spectrum and not concerned with gay issues at all, then we've really achieved something," reasoned May. "Because the young kids who follow Guns N' Roses and heavy metal will sit up and realize that this concerns them too…

"I'm a big fan of Axl," May went on. "The fact that he speaks honestly about being scared by gays, for one thing, is actually very valuable, and because he said, 'I'm doing this because I feel for Freddie and because I feel that this issue involves everybody'.

"Axl was able to look privately at his own feelings… about why he was afraid of gays; now he's much more at home with himself. So there you have a person who's growing up and coming in tune with his own feelings—and he's doing it publicly, which is a pretty dangerous thing to do."

As it turned out, Guns N' Roses' performance

Fashion–conscious Axl rocks out in a leather kilt.

went without too much of a hitch—the only problem came in having to trim their scheduled three-song set to two (ditching 'Sweet Child O'Mine') but at least they hadn't over-run to squeeze the extra song in. Their brief slot mixed the optimistic with the sombre, combining a glimpse of bright skies via 'Paradise City' with the downbeat power of Bob Dylan's 'Knocking On Heaven's Door'—a song they seemed determined to make their own.

COMIN' ON

But for the 70,000 fans at Wembley and a massive worldwide television audience, Guns N' Roses' most significant contribution came when they loosened up and joined in the celebration of Mercury and his music. Slash traded hot guitar licks with Brian May as the remaining trio of Queen members (with Joe Elliott of Def Leppard on vocals) blitzed through the punchy 'Tie Your Mother Down'—though it was Axl who was really to steal the show later in the evening.

A succession of superstars had performed Queen classics ranging from dynamic rock material (courtesy of Robert Plant, Extreme, Metallica and others) through the bizarre (Annie Lennox and David Bowie on the Queen/Bowie duet 'Under Pressure') to the soulful (with George Michael and Lisa Stansfield).

Mercury's close friend Elton John led the crowd through the introductory part of Queen's epic 'Bohemian Rhapsody'. But following the melodramatic mock-opera of the mid-section, as the band surged into the distinctive hard rock riff of the climax, it was Axl who came running from the wings to take over the vocals—sending the crowd wild.

For the song's gentle coda, Elton John joined Rose at the front of the stage to duet the sentiment "nothing really matters…" Serious Guns N' Roses aficionados would have been aware of Rose's enthusiasm for John's early work. But for most, the moment was highly charged—here was Elton John, self-proclaimed bisexual and dedicated campaigner for AIDS charities, in a seemingly uneasy truce with Rose, whose attitude to homosexuality was seen as openly hostile.

As the pair wound down Queen's most bombastic of songs, neither seemed quite sure how to react to the other, and the sense of vague unease was spine tingling. Axl later claimed that "if you look close, you can see how much love and respect I have for Elton". In truth the emotions running between the two seemed a lot more complex. But by the time they made —admittedly tentative—physical contact, it was clear just how far Axl had come from being the baddest boy in town, on the Sunset Strip.

SONS OF THE STRIP

Sunset Boulevard is an artery of dreams, aspirations and despair that runs through the very heart of Los Angeles—from the fresh spray of the Pacific Ocean to the Latin-American ghettos of east Los Angeles. They call the west Hollywood section the Sunset Strip. It's where aspirant rock stars in beat-up vans make their pilgrimage to play at famed rock joints like the Whiskey A Go Go and the Roxy. On the way there, they'll cruise alongside the movers and shakers of the

Los Angeles, the city of dreams

music industry, driving west up Sunset towards the headquarters of Geffen Records, or east towards Hollywood and the Capitol Records building. The idea is that with the music industry on your doorstep, your chances of being signed up by an A&R man are that much higher.

They pack bands in tight at clubs like the Roxy. Like aeroplanes stacked by air traffic controllers over jam-packed runways, the rock bands of LA circle the

The Whiskey A Go Go club, on LA's famed Sunset Strip

Strip until a slot becomes available. With hundreds of bands competing, wily promoters cram five or more a night into the crucial clubs. The pay-to-play system means that bands are expected to buy, then resell, tickets for their own shows and most end up discounting or giving them away and making a loss.

While waiting for the big break, bands push promotional flyers into any hand that'll take them, and rub shoulders with the lucky few who have played the system and won, in the low, low lighting of a restaurant hang out like the Rainbow Bar & Grill.

> "IN SOME WAYS I HATE THE WAY I WAS RAISED... THE LACK OF SUPPORT FOR ANYTHING I WAS INTO OR GOOD AT. BUT IN A WAY I CAN'T HATE IT, BECAUSE IT GAVE ME THIS SENSE OF DRIVE...THIS MISSION TO DO SOMETHING WITH MY LIFE."
> **Axl**

Young punks go for it—an early live gig

advertising space in the local rock rags and investing in prime pay-to-play slots in the clubs. The less fortunate take menial jobs to fuel the rock'n'roll habit and live in cheap apartments—or girlfriends' apartments. Exploiting gullible girlfriends becomes a way of life, doing whatever it takes to get ahead and anything to get noticed.

They say the Sunset Strip is dead now. The grunge-rock capital of Seattle has eclipsed LA as the breeding ground for major-league rock'n'roll, a change that can be largely laid at the feet of world-beaters Nirvana and Pearl Jam. But in the late Eighties, the Sunset Strip was the only place to be. A fact not lost on two escapees from the arid nothingness of Lafayette, Indiana—Bill Bailey and Jeff

Then there are Sunset's other landmarks—the Sunset Strip Tattoo parlour; the Continental Hyatt hotel, renamed the 'Riot' by one-time regular hell-raising residents Led Zeppelin; and LA's Tower Records, purveying the fruits of the record industry late into the night. The Sunset Strip is Mecca for every would-be hustler and hobo muso in America.

The lucky ones live off allowances provided by indulgent parents, buying the best equipment,

> **"I HAVE A TENDENCY TO GET REALLY DRUNK AND THEN I GET TO THE HOTEL AND I'LL PICK UP THE FIRST CHICK I CAN GET"**
> *Slash*

Isbell. Their exodus to LA and the trials and tribulations they endured are hardly unique. But, reborn as W Axl Rose and Izzy Stradlin, they shook LA like an earthquake.

Meet Guns N' Roses, born and raised on Sunset Strip.

MISPLACED CHILDHOODS

Before Bill Bailey became the flame-haired hoodlum W Axl Rose, he experienced a childhood as emotionally crippling as they come. Born in Lafayette, Indiana, on February 6, 1962, Bill was raised by his mother, Sharon Bailey and L Stephen Bailey, the man he had been led to believe was his real father. In fact, Axl's true father, William Rose, had abandoned his wife and child when his son was only two. At the age of 17, the delinquent youth discovered his true parentage and changed his name. Enter W Rose ("William," he decided, "was an asshole"—a conclusion which accounted for the blunt abbreviation).

An early association with the Pentecostal Church, where Bill sang and even taught Sunday School, only added to a slow-burning anger and sexual confusion.

Where did you get that coat? Axl was always a snappy dresser.

He'd been taught to believe women were evil: "I remember the first time I got smacked for looking at a woman… it was a cigarette advertisement with two girls coming out of the water in bikinis. I was just staring at the TV—not thinking, just watching—and my dad smacked me in the mouth… the Bible was shoved down my throat, and it really distorted my point of view."

In an article that appeared after he'd found success, Axl made a shocking revelation which added sexual abuse to this heady cocktail of old-style religion, identity crisis and domestic violence. In an interview with Rolling Stone magazine in early 1992, he claimed that intensive therapy sessions had enabled him to examine parts of his life that he'd previously suppressed.

"Basically, I've been rejected by my mother since I was a baby," he told reporter Kim Neely. "She's picked my stepfather over me ever since he was around and watched me get beaten by him."

Asked about his biological father, William Rose, he explained that "my mom's eyes actually turn black whenever it's brought up how terrible this person was."

At the age of two, claimed Axl, his father kidnapped him. "I remember being sexually abused by this man and watching something horrible happen to my mother when she came to get me. I don't know all the details… I got a lot of violent, abusive thoughts towards women out of watching my mom with this man."

BRIGHT LIGHTS, BIG CITY

Inevitably, this bright but volatile youth made trouble for himself. With a trail of minor offences behind him, the increasingly wayward W Rose left town—probably

Izzy, a major league Keith Richard fan, meets the man himself.

Mike Monroe, the Hanoi Rocks man who provided so much visual inspiration.

to the relief of the local police. His destination was LA. A rough-neck hayseed kid from the sticks, Rose rode a Greyhound bus into a world that jolted him like an electric shock. "When I lived in Indiana I was labelled a punk… a punk rocker," said Axl. "When I moved to LA, the punks called me a hippy and didn't want anything to do with me. The Hollywood rock scene was a war-zone back then. I tried out for a punk band and I didn't make it because they said I sounded like Robert Plant."

He quickly hooked up with another Indiana exile, Jeff Isbell—two months his junior and also trying to shake the torpor of the town he called "Bumfuck, Indiana" from his bones. According to Izzy, "the first thing I remember about Axl—before I really knew him—is the first day of class, eighth or ninth grade, I'm sitting in class and I hear this noise going on in front… and then there's this scuffle and then I see him, Axl, and this teacher bouncing off a door jamb. And then Axl was gone down the hall with all these teachers running after him."

Jeff, or Izzy Stradlin, as he preferred to call himself, had a definitive vision. At first glance, he

New York Dolls—proto-glamour-punks and an early influence

could have been one of a million young Keith Richards clones, but along with a love of low-slung Rolling Stones riffola, Stradlin also had a taste for fist-in-your-face punk rock. Izzy wanted a band with the gut-level groove of the former and the no-nonsense intensity of the later. He even knew how he wanted the band to look.

His chief visual inspiration came from Hanoi Rocks—a cult Finnish garage-rock combo who themselves owed a debt to the whole New York Dolls/Johnny Thunders glamour-junkie axis. A far cry from the LA rock style of Barbie doll glam and spandex rockers, Hanoi favoured the teddy boy kind of drape jackets and brothel creepers. It was a sleazier, yet suaver look.

Stradlin, Rose and a guitarist called Chris Weber formed the nucleus of a band called AXL. The name was annexed by W Rose after the band ditched it— once rechristened Axl Rose, his new name also doubled as an anagram for 'oral sex'!

A ROCK'N'ROLL APPRENTICESHIP

They stepped on to the treadmill of the LA club scene at a bar in the San Fernando Valley called the Orphanage. Chris Weber was happy to take life as it came, blasting out simple punk'n'roll tunes that owed more to the Ramones than the big-selling metal acts of the day. "For me it was just an excuse to adopt the lifestyle," explained Weber. "But they [Axl and Izzy] were really motivated by the idea of being big rock stars. I mean, I was into playing my guitar, but shopping for a record deal wasn't my primary goal in life."

Out on the streets, G N' R very much at home

Axl's big hair explosion

Izzy and Axl had focus—Axl even used to quote from a guide book on how to succeed in the music industry. And according to Weber, Rose was "always throwing shit-fits". The AXL band soon changed its name to Rose, before changing again to Hollywood Rose. With drummer Johnny Christ and bassist Andre Troxx in tow (attention grabbing names were essential on the club circuit), Hollywood Rose eventually disintegrated at a gig in Santa Monica. Not much was left in the rubble apart from a song called 'Anything Goes' for which Weber retained a co-writing credit—

> "AT TIMES I ENJOY WRITING AND AT OTHER TIMES I JUST HATE IT BECAUSE IT'S DEFINITELY HAVING TO GO BACK AND EXPERIENCE SOME PAIN AND EXPRESS HOW YOU REALLY FEEL."
>
> *Axl*

after much conflict with Axl.

Axl attempted to get it on with another local club act who were to attain some minor success, LA Guns, but that failed to ignite. Izzy passed briefly through a band of veteran nobodies called London, whose other ex-members included WASP's Blackie Lawless and Motley Crüe's Nikki Sixx (which says more about the ebb and flow of musicians from one LA band to another than it does about London).

With nothing exciting on the horizon, Axl, Izzy and Weber staged a Hollywood Rose reunion, drafting in a bassist called Steve Darrow and drummer Rob Gardner. They played a 1984 New Year's Eve show in San Pedro, before Weber drifted off and Tracii Guns of LA Guns drifted in—the two band's names wouldn't be combined until later in 1985. The band was nominally a club-scene supergroup by now, though the set up was really just another permutation of local musicians struggling for the right combination.

Then there was a similar band called Road Crew which most of the time only really consisted of a drummer and a guitarist. Their sticks man Steven Adler, though born in Cleveland, Ohio, had reinvented himself as a sun-bleached, totally-uncomplicated Californian rocker, while the guitarist was Adler's old school friend Saul Hudson, son of a black, American clothes-designing mother and an English graphic-

> "I THINK WE'VE COME UP WITH A SOUND THAT'S PRETTY INTERESTING. IT'S GOT SOME ELEMENTS THAT PEOPLE CAN RECOGNIZE, BUT WE'RE NOT RIPPING ANYONE OFF."
> *Axl*

artist father. Hudson was an energetic, BMX-bike racing kid nicknamed 'Slash' because he was forever whizzing around the place.

Saul 'Slash' Hudson had been born in Stoke-on-Trent, England. His mother Ola had designed stage costumes for the likes of David Bowie—with whom she had an affair after she was separated from her husband—and his father had designed record sleeves for prestigious artists such as Neil Young.

Tracii Guns gave the band half their name but left soon after.

Slash's was an unconventional childhood. He'd been brought up around an eclectic range of musical influences, playing records belonging to his parents and had been allowed to roam free.

GOING TO CALIFORNIA

When he moved with his father to Los Angeles at the age of 12, he continued exploring his rare freedoms, dabbling with drink and observing the comings and goings of the various celebrities who drifted through the family home. He soon hooked up with the skateboarding Adler, and the two young teens skipped school, hung out and practiced a little guitar at Stevie's grandmother's place. Baffled by the instrument, but fired by Adler's rudimentary attempts

We were the Road Crew—big buddies Slash and Steven chill together.

to play, Slash gave it a go himself and eventually surpassed Adler's two-chord talents by sheer trial and error.

The pair got a little more serious when Adler moved over to the drum stool and even though it still

> "WITH US, IT'S A REAL BLOOD, SWEAT AND TEARS TYPE THING. WE HAVE A GREAT TIME WHEN WE'RE PLAYING AND WE GO THROUGH A LOT OF HARD TIMES."
> *Slash*

only existed in their minds, Road Crew was born. Slash meandered through a couple of local outfits, and rehearsed for others, but he always returned to Stevie, cheap booze and Road Crew jams in the garage. Slash had even auditioned for Guns N' Roses along the way, but according to Axl, "he was too bluesy at the time and too good—we thought he was too far into what he was doing, and we wouldn't be able to relate".

Mostly, he and Adler divided their enthusiasm in equal amounts between Road Crew—"a great little band," he claimed, "sort of like Metallica are now, but without a singer"—and getting wasted. The vital link between the Axl/Izzy camp and the Slash/Adler corner was to come in the lanky shape of Michael 'Duff' McKagan.

PUNK DRIFTER

The youngest of eight children, McKagan had played in numerous bands in his home town of Seattle—he's always quick to point out that it wasn't just punk bands, but the notion of McKagan as teen punkster seems to have stuck. Flexible enough to play drums, bass or guitar to the minimal level required to join bands like the Fartz or Ten Minute Warning, Duff drifted from band to band and instrument to instrument. He even rehearsed on drums with minor British punk survivors the Angelic Upstarts when they

Slash shows what he's made of with another scorching solo.

> **"THERE'S A TIME TO DO DRUGS AND A TIME TO DRINK AND THERE'S A TIME TO DO WHAT YOU'VE GOT TO DO... AND YOU'VE GOT TO REALIZE THE DIFFERENCE."**
> *Duff*

passed through Seattle.

Bands from Seattle just weren't getting the record deals back in the days before the likes of Nirvana took off, so he followed the goldrush trail to LA. An acquaintance pointed him in the direction of Slash, who disappointingly failed to live up to what Duff assumed to be a punk rock nickname. Still, one metal-head/hippie guitarist and a slightly irritating hard rock drummer were better than nothing, so he gave Road Crew a spin. Then, sensing that Road Crew were a band in name only, he moved a small step up the LA scene's food chain and joined Guns N' Roses on bass.

Pretty in pink? Duff in a daze

GUNS AND ROAD CREW

Duff used his old punk contacts to book a tour for his new band. But at the last minute before the first date (an LA show at the Troubador on Santa Monica Boulevard), guitarist Tracii Guns and drummer Rob Gardner decided that they couldn't be bothered with the hassle of playing out of town. Rather than cancel the dates, Duff suggested recruiting Road Crew's core duo as replacements. With nothing better to do, Adler and Slash learned the Guns N' Roses set as best they could in 48 hours and the tour was on—almost…

The band set out for Seattle in a borrowed car, with a couple of buddies roped in as roadies. Barely 100 miles out of LA, the car broke down. The band attempted to hitch-hike but, looking like the rockers they were, found few takers. The journey took them two and a half days in the end. Once in Seattle they managed to borrow equipment and play a basic show anyway, but received a less than inspiring response:

"There were 10, maybe 20 people there," according to Izzy. While their roadies were struggling to fix the car and meet them in Seattle, they decided to abandon this 'Hell Tour' and high-tailed it back to LA, where their performance at the Troubador had

Don't stand so close to me—Axl and Duff in a tight situation

made a big enough impression to win them a regular, Monday night gig.

Road Crew were going nowhere, so it made sense for Adler and Slash to hitch up with the Guns N' Roses posse. The 'Hell Tour' had cemented friendships within the band and suddenly the chemistry was right. Guns N' Roses set about making

Poison—G N' R's arch rivals on the LA club scene

a stink, with Slash making a token effort to carry though the band's gutter-slut look with a smear of lipstick (the *Live ?!*@ Like A Suicide* sleeve features incriminating photographic evidence).

> **"WE KNOW WE'RE ALWAYS GOING TO BE AT ODDS WITH PEOPLE ON SOMETHING. A LOT OF PEOPLE ARE AFRAID TO BE THAT WAY WE'RE NOT."**
> *Axl*

The band were still gnawing away at the club scene but their reputation was growing at last. With more acts on the circuit adopting a polished glam-rock look, Guns N' Roses were hell bent on setting their own agenda. Though Izzy in particular had put a lot of thought into how the band should look, Guns N' Roses cultivated the impression that they didn't give a damn—anti-style as an attitude. Lest anyone should confuse their garbage-can chic with the rhinestone glitz of Poison and their ilk, Axl

Meet our idols—Axl with Steven Tyler of Aerosmith

scrawled the legend 'Glam Sucks' on one trouser leg.

POISONED ROSE

Poison emerged as Guns N' Roses's arch rivals. Slash had auditioned for them early on, but was unable to fit in with their maximum make-up look. The real rivalry developed when both bands played the same clubs—Poison resorted to underhand tactics to steal the crowd. "Some nights they'd come on first, some nights we would," remembered Slash. "But every time those assholes played first, Bret Michaels [Poison's frontman] would end their set by announcing that the band were having a big party somewhere and everybody was invited. And, man, the people who frequent the sort of dives we were playing in those days didn't need to be asked twice… Within minutes, the club would be empty!"

All's fair in love and music but, for Gun N' Roses, Poison had come to represent everything that was fake about a hard rock scene increasingly geared towards looking good on MTV.

LIVING ROUGH

Away from the struggle to make their name on stage, Guns N' Roses spent the first half of 1986 roughing it in a tiny hole of a rehearsal studio on Gardener Street, where the five of them lived as well as

Nazareth—strange but true, an early influence on G N' R

practiced. "We tried to live on $3.75 (£2.50 at current rates) a day, which was enough to buy biscuits and gravy at Denny's for a buck and a quarter. Or some really cheap wine like Thunderbird," recalled Axl. "It was, like, 19 per cent alcohol and one bottle of that… Even if you're dead tired you made a party. And a packet of cigarettes. That's it. We survived." It was a familiar route to success for a rock band. The fliers they circulated took a blunt approach to extolling the band's down-to-earth virtues: "Straight out of detox—only the strong survive."

Their new headquarters—dubbed 'Hellhouse'—operated an open-door policy for assorted hangers-on to party, guzzle booze and maybe score some soft drugs. They packed the place out with floozies and groupies, and made the best of a bad situation. "It didn't have a shower," reported Axl. "The rain always leaked in. I once stole this wood and we built this loft so we could have a place to sleep above the equipment. We tried to get in as many girls as we could. It all got pretty wild. There was a lot of indoor and outdoor sex."

Despite the distractions, the band's sound was beginning to ferment into something with as much punch as the gut-rot wine they were so fond of. As Axl put it, they were "a sore thumb on the glam scene—in the middle of it, but at the same time not into it at all".

They even had a manager of sorts, one Vicki Hamilton—a local scenester who'd helped book some gigs, stored their equipment and promised to raise

The look that set G N' R aside from the LA mainstream.

some much-needed capital for the band. And the record labels were starting to sniff round. One talent scout, Tom Zutaut, had already signed archetypical LA shock-rock combo Motley Crüe to Elektra Records. Now working for Geffen Records, he was setting about building the hard-rock roster for that

Axl putting the Hanoi influence into action.

Hot and sweaty and ready for anything

label too. Guns N' Roses and Zutaut spoke the same language—most of the other labels did not. The band were happy to be wined and dined by would-be suitors, but most experiences quickly confirmed their worst fears about the music industry.

On the other hand Geffen were, according to Izzy "the coolest—they were very hip to what was going on. They knew about rock'n'roll… At one label something came up about Steven Tyler [Aerosmith vocalist] and this chick said 'Who's that?'"

Having inked a deal in March 1986, Geffen wanted to bring Guns N' Roses under the wing of an established manager. Zutaut and the band had little luck persuading the likes of Doug Thaler (Motley Crüe) or Tim Collins (Aerosmith) that Guns N' Roses spelled anything other than trouble. Meanwhile, their old manager, Vicki Hamilton, decided to sue the band to recoup an alleged investment she'd made in them. Later Geffen and the band were to settle out of court

King rockers—is this the "classic" line-up?

for $30,000 (£20,000).

Alan Niven, manager of LA act Great White, eventually took the reins. Niven had no great expectations of Guns N' Roses, but he was a hard grafter and they liked his straight-talking attitude, and he did his best to make them knuckle down to work on their first album.

WELCOME TO THE STUDIO

Before any recording could be done, a producer had to be chosen. It was easier said than done. One rarely-acknowledged influence on the Guns N' Roses

Guns N' Roses—one band, one attitude

possible producer when we got signed. That didn't quite work out because we had different ideas."

"We wasted a lot of money flying this guy from Scotland to LA…" complained Izzy. "Slash and I drove through some valley, what did he say? 'Guys, this car hasn't been serviced for a while, has it?' Cars aren't serviced in America, you just buy an old thing for $100. I loved him, but he was too scared…"

Another candidate for production chores was Paul Stanley, frontman with US rock institution Kiss. But

An early appearance for Axl's famous head-band

sound is Scottish band Nazareth, whose singer Dan McCafferty has a leather-lunged vocal style that Guns N' Roses fans may find eerily familiar. Said Axl: "It was 'Love Hurts', the Nazareth version, that got me singing in my high voice… In fact we flew Manny [Charlton], the guitarist from Nazareth, over as a

> **"THE FIRST RECORD WON'T HAVE CERTAIN THINGS THAT THE SECOND RECORD WILL HAVE, BECAUSE IT'S NOT THE RIGHT TIME YET. WE HAVE TO HELP KNOCK DOWN A COUPLE OF DOORS."**
> **Axl**

> "IN A WORLD HE DID NOT CREATE, HE WILL GO THROUGH IT AS IF IT WERE HIS OWN MAKING: HALF MAN, HALF BEAST, I DON'T KNOW WHAT IT IS BUT IT'S WEIRD AND IT'S PISSED OFF AND IT CALLS ITSELF SLASH."
> *Axl*

the band felt he didn't understand them—his sacrilegious suggestion that he rewrite a couple of their songs didn't go down well. And Spencer Proffer, who'd produced Quiet Riot's *Metal Health*, a massive hard-rock hit album of the early Eighties, similarly failed to impress.

Mick Clink, a mid-ranking recording

Axl's Keith Richard t-shirt warns of the danger of drugs— or is it just a joke?

PATIENCE PLEASE... A DRUG FREE AMERICA COMES FIRST!

engineer, took to the producer's chair in the end and the band attempted to slam down some tracks. They found themselves hindered by the deteriorating conditions of Izzy and Slash, who'd slid from dabbling with heroin into full-blown junkiedom.

With growing anxiety, Geffen watched their new signings stall on the starting blocks. In order to sustain a street buzz Geffen decided to put out an EP of live tracks. Released for extra gritty effect on a pseudo-indie label called Uzi Suicide (complete with cheapo sleeve courtesy of Slash), *Live ?!*@ Like A Suicide* encapsulated the simple, cranked-up appeal of Guns N' Roses. Gnarly opener 'Reckless Life' quickly established one of Axl's recurring themes, spitting in the eye of authority. The other original, 'Move To The City', highlighted another obsession—fear and alienation. Covers of Australian hard-nut rockers Rose Tattoo's 'Nice Boys (Don't Play Rock'N'Roll…)' and Aerosmith's snotty 'Mama Kin' completed this freeze-frame snapshot of the band in

On the road or off, Slash always had time to make new friends.

action—and there were 10,000 vinyl copies of the EP to whet the appetite of both the hard-rock press and the quickly growing fan base.

Once the album proper was finally in the can, Niven roped in a sympathetic publicist, one Arlette Vereeke, and sent the band to London. They set up in a cramped apartment off London's Kensington High

Duff 'n' Izzy sing the G N' R blues

Street and got on with doing what they still do best—making that Guns N' Roses noise.

Axl almost didn't make it, allegedly finding himself in hospital after a beating from the LA Police Department and a course of electroshock therapy treatment. "I got hit on the head by a cop and I guess I just blacked out," he's supposed to have said. "Two days later I woke up in hospital."

WEA records, Geffen's UK distributor at the time, were unimpressed by these scummy reprobates with

> "ALL OF A SUDDEN I'M DIAGNOSED MANIC-DEPRESSIVE... 'LET'S PUT AXL ON MEDICATION'. WELL THE MEDICATION DOESN'T HELP ME DEAL WITH THE STRESS. THE ONLY THING IT DOES IS KEEP PEOPLE OFF MY BACK."
> *Axl*

no album ready for promotion. They still released a taster single, pairing the frantically f-word-littered 'It's So Easy', with their ode to heroin hang-ups, 'Mr. Brownstone' (12-inch copies also contained 'Move To The City', plus 'Shadow Of Your Love'—a rare, otherwise-unreleased bruiser from the *Live ?!*@ Like A Suicide* sessions).

The first of three shows at London's Marquee Club misfired badly. The crowd greeted them with a hail of beer glasses and spit and, with the band somewhat shaken up, reviewers concluded they'd blown it. But a solid performance three days later got them back on track and by the end of their visit, a show on June 28, 1987, they were looking like the stuff of legends—lewd, crude and viciously effective. In between times, the band fraternized with and terrorized various rock hacks (as Niven hoped they would) and generally behaved like gung-ho gate-crashers. Whatever this phenomenon from the States was, it wasn't putting on its best manners for a first visit overseas to Britain: Axl risked arrest when, jet-lagged and drowsy on hay-fever tablets, he almost passed out on the steps of Tower Records in London—security guards who attempted to move him on discovered he wasn't too sedated to retaliate…

Slash survives daylight!

WAKE UP, TIME TO DIE

"You know where you are? You're in the jungle baby, you're gonna d-i-i-i-e-e-e!" This gloating, banshee wail delivered midway through 'Welcome To The Jungle', the opening track of Guns N' Roses' debut album, is the band marking out its territory. *Appetite For Destruction* showcases a gang of bad-attitude punk-metallers with sneers like switchblades, ready to rub your nose in their world—the grimy streets of LA's underbelly repainted a nightmarish blood-red.

Throughout *Appetite For Destruction*, Axl swings like a pendulum between hedonistic predator and persecuted escapee. Recurring themes of violation, nihilistic self-destruction and a voyeuristic fascination with the most sordid, lowlife existence dominate, with that desire for escape as an undercurrent. Candidly autobiographical, Axl's lyrics lay bare the soul of the band.

"'My Michelle' is a true story," he explained. "'Rocket Queen', I'm singing it as if it's me but it's about this girl I know and I'm singing as though I was in her shoes, and then at the end of the song I am, like, singing a song to her because she is a friend of mine. 'Think About You' is about a girl I used to go out with. 'Sweet Child O'Mine' is about my girlfriend right now. The whole record is about someone we've known and hung out with or something we've done. It's not like a fantasy picture from a distance."

Musically, *Appetite For Destruction* couldn't be

> ## "IT'S SO BASIC TO ME AND IT'S REALLY HARD TO EXPLAIN. YOU GET IN THERE WRITING AND YOU THINK YOU'RE THE WORST SONGWRITER IN THE WORLD, AND THEN YOU WRITE ONE COOL TUNE, LIKE 'JUNGLE'..."
> ### Slash

Axl's tattoo became the alternative *Appetite* sleeve.

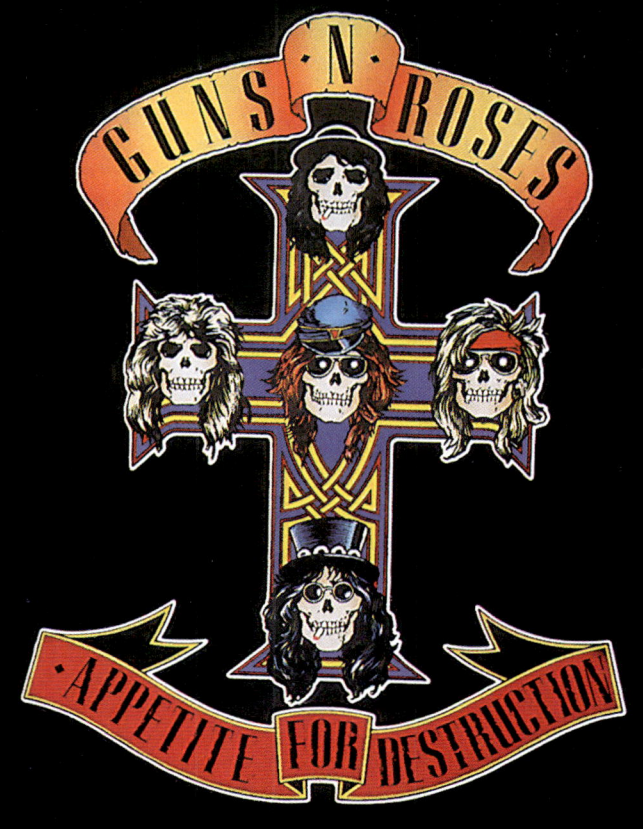

Faster Pussycat—another LA club band and occasional Guns support act

right and centre.

Before Guns N' Roses, heavy rock represented many things—excessive volume, flashy showmanship, wide-screen heroics—but any element of danger was caged in theatricality. Guns N' Roses offered the real deal—scumlife values allied to a brutal musical virtuosity. They quickly laid claim to the title 'Most Dangerous Band In The World'—and the reputation was clearly deserved.

Within a year or two, virtually every band in Los Angeles was trying to emulate Guns N' Roses's scuzzball chic. Chins which had spent years behind carefully applied foundation suddenly sported stubble; pristine arms acquired hastily applied tattoos. Everyone wanted a slice of Guns N' Roses' charisma. But that moment, in the summer of 1987, was strictly their own.

NOT WITH A WHIMPER

Appetite For Destruction may have exploded like a nail bomb as far as the hard-rock press were concerned, but the rest of the world was undisturbed. The sleeve which gave the record its name—a 1978 painting by hot-rod artist Robert Williams of an avenging red devil attacking a robot seemingly caught after an act of rape—had caused a few disapproving glances. Soon, the record company was offering

faulted. Though Slash claimed that 'Sweet Child O'Mine' began life almost as a joke, both that track and the spirit-raising 'Paradise City' showed true songwriting craftsmanship. And it wasn't just Axl who impressed: Duff's bass, chunky and up-front, rang out like a lead instrument; Adler's drums beat a frantic tattoo; Izzy handled the rhythm chops like a trooper; and Slash unleashed deadly, mercurial guitar left,

materialize as US interest in Aerosmith was soaring, so the 'Smiths blew out their European dates to concentrate on their American revival. The Aerosmith bookings were no club dates, they were sizeable concert halls and Guns N' Roses audaciously announced that they would headline a scaled-down version of the tour. At some of the provincial dates attendances were just average at best but in London, where their summer sojourn had made a definite impression, they all but sold out the prestigious

retailers an alternative image, based on the band as a tattoo of a cross formed by their skulls. Gimmicks aside, the best way for the band to get known was to get down to some serious touring—and it was to be a prestigious outing.

The Cult's Ian Astbury had seen Guns N' Roses at one of their Marquee dates, and was impressed: they were welcomed on his band's US tour. As they got into the swing of their first major jaunt, an even more enticing pairing seemed to be in the offing—a UK tour with the original masters of disaster, Aerosmith. But this potentially lethal link failed to

Note the drummer—it's Fred Coury of Cinderella, not Steven.

Hammersmith Odeon (now the Labatt's Apollo).

As ever, the more responsive the crowd, the better the band's performance. At Nottingham's Rock City, Guns N' Roses rewarded rabid enthusiasm with an equally feral show; without similar feedback from

Party animals! Steven Adler with fellow drummer Tommy Lee of Motley Crüe

a sparse Manchester crowd the band fizzled out in little over an hour. In London they gave what amounted to a homecoming show of euphoric ferocity. As a tie-in with the tour, 'Welcome To The Jungle' was released as a single and scraped into the lower end of the UK charts.

Support band on the tour had been Faster Pussycat, fellow LA sleazeballs who were never quite able to step out of Guns N' Roses' shadow. In fact few —if any—of the bands signed up to be the next Guns N' Roses saw any real long-term success. And it wasn't a manufactured success, either. Though the band had secured some influential supporters in the UK press, the notion that Guns N' Roses were universally hyped is quite wrong. An early interview in *Metal Hammer* magazine took a particularly hostile tone, and Axl defended the band's *Appetite For Destruction* album by bizarrely declaring "the EP's a piece of shit compared to the album… that's the most contrived piece of shit we've done yet. It ain't a live

Thinking that no one's looking, Slash sneaks a quick drink.

record—if you think it is, you're crazy. What we did was go into a room, record ourselves and put 50,000 screaming people on top".

FLIRTING WITH DISASTER

The next logical step was a higher-profile US tour. Enter Motley Crüe who were currently riding high in the charts with their *Girls, Girls, Girls* album. They'd pioneered the LA hard-rock scene at the beginning of the Eighties and were accustomed to partying as hard

Motley Crüe—Steven and Slash saw Nikki overdose, then singer Vince started a war of words with Axl.

as Guns N' Roses. But when reminded that their manager Doug Thaler had turned down Guns N' Roses in early 1986, anyone would think it strange that this recipe for doom was allowed to lurch out onto the road…

Steven Adler was an early casualty, boozily punching a lamp post outside a bar in Michigan and breaking his hand. The band's performance suffered with stand-in drummer Fred Coury, of Cinderella (Slash felt Coury couldn't follow the band's instinctive tempo changes), but their ability to party, particularly with Crüe bassist Nikki Sixx, remained undiminished.

Guns N' Roses were warned by Motley's management that further 'bad behaviour' would result in eviction from the tour. But the partying continued after the lamp post incident until the fateful night when Adler and Slash stumbled in on Sixx who had overdosed on heroin in his hotel room. By calling an ambulance and pushing Sixx under a cold shower the Guns N' Roses pair saved his life. But, with Motley's management trying to suppress the story, rumours emerged heaping blame on Gun N' Roses—emphasizing their general 'bad influence' instead of crediting them for the intervention.

More roadwork with Alice Cooper followed after this disastrous outing, along with some hometown shows. This wasn't easy work either and included one gig at LA club the Cathouse where Axl was arrested for an alleged assault on a security guard. The band limped on without him and vocals were handled by Izzy.

In the New Year, they headlined a short US tour with English pseudo-bikers Zodiac Mindwarp and the Love Reaction in support, which led to disorder on a daily basis. In Phoenix, Arizona, Axl apparently quit and further infuriated Slash by locking himself in his hotel room. But after a few uneasy days Axl and Slash patched things up and the band spent a while knocking songs together in the studio. The acoustic-based sessions included 'Used To Love Her (But I Had To Kill Her)' which was a throwaway bar-room strum-along that fuelled their reputation for blatant sexism (it was later covered as a B-side by LA all-girl rockers L7 as 'Used To Love Him'). There was also a moody, slowed-down version of 'You're Crazy', and

> **"I DON'T KNOW ANY MORE WHAT PEOPLE EXPECT FROM US. THEY SEEM TO BE WAITING TO SEE WHAT WE'LL DO NEXT. I FEEL AS IF I'M WALKING AROUND IN A CIRCUS ACT ALL DAY..."**
> *Slash*

> **"IT'S A GREAT FEELING BEING UP THERE AND BEING RESPECTED FOR BEING A GOOD ROCK'N'ROLL BAND. IT MAKES IT ALL WORTHWHILE WHEN WE GO THROUGH ALL THE SHIT THAT WE GET ON A DAILY BASIS ON A PERSONAL LEVEL."**
> *Slash*

Iron Maiden celebrate the news that G N' R are off their tour.

'Patience'—a simple, sensitive ballad of Izzy's.

With the album sales finally moving into a higher gear and 'Sweet Child O'Mine' scaling the singles charts, the touring continued with another unlikely pairing—this time with ultra-traditional heavy-metal act Iron Maiden. While Guns N' Roses were too similar to Motley Crüe for their own good, their high octane antics failed to endear themselves to the stoical British headliners—they were just too different. To add to the problems, Duff got married mid-tour to girlfriend Mandy Brix and his stand-in—from Zodiac Mindwarp and, briefly, the Cult—was Haggis, otherwise known as Kid Chaos. By his own admission Haggis made a hopeless replacement. The band eventually withdrew from the tour, with Axl claiming throat problems (the indignity of opening for Iron Maiden at two Californian venues might also have had something to do with it).

But there was no doubt that Guns N' Roses had moved into a bigger league—their heroes had become their friends.

ROCKIN' WITH THEIR HEROES

"When I started getting into rock'n'roll on my own—outside of my family's influences—what inspired me to play guitar was something that happened when I was 13," explained Slash. "I chased the most beautiful girl—who was twice my age—for about three months.

Cinderella, with short-lived G N' R drummer Fred Coury second from the right

And when I finally got into her apartment, she played me *Rocks* for the first time. I listened to it about four or five times, completely forgot about the girl and split the apartment. That's what Aerosmith means to me."

Aerosmith were to the Seventies what Guns N' Roses were to become in the Nineties—the biggest white-trash stadium rock attraction in America. Symbolically, the duo at the heart of Aerosmith—the now clean-living singer Steven Tyler and guitarist Joe Perry—presented Slash with a T-shirt bearing their 'bad old days' nickname: The Toxic Twins. Even

Aerosmith seemed happy to hail Guns N' Roses as the new standard bearers for mainline decadent rock'n'roll when the two bands finally got their tour together. But the good times for Guns N' Roses were curtailed by a firm ruling designed to keep all drink and drugs away from Aerosmith's strictly sober members, though business as usual was maintained

> **"AEROSMITH ARE A TRADITION THAT I GREW UP WITH. THEY WERE THE ONLY BAND THAT THE PEOPLE WHO LIVED IN MY CITY IN INDIANA WOULD ACCEPT WEARING MAKE-UP AND DRESSED COOL."**
> *Axl*

within their own dressing room.

The tour took the band through the summer of 1988 with the usual roll call of minor skirmishes, including the time Axl punched out a businessman in a Chicago hotel for committing the heinous crime of referring to him as a Bon Jovi lookalike, and another incident when he thumped a parking lot attendant in Philadelphia. On both occasions he enjoyed a quick

On stage at Donington, where tragedy soured the day

Slash, who says he'll never forget the Donington deaths.

look at the inside of a police cell.

THEIR DARKEST DAY

Public demand meant a return to the UK was inevitable and Guns N' Roses were booked for the prestigious Monsters Of Rock festival at Castle Donington. On the day the band would jet in on Concorde—Alan Niven's idea, considered a cool touch by Slash—play the show, then return to the US and more dates with Aerosmith.

Guns N' Roses' own slot was second from bottom, beneath Megadeth, Kiss, David Lee Roth and the headliners Iron Maiden, and reflected both the overall strength of the line-up—considered to be the most impressive in the festival's history—and the fact that Guns N' Roses's success had caught many unawares. By the time Saturday, August 20 arrived, the anticipation of those who had never seen these exotic creatures from LA had reached a crescendo. The weather was poor but the crowd was swelling towards a record attendance officially recorded as 98,000. The wind was strong enough to blow over a large video screen and rain battered both stage and fans as German heavy-metal act Helloween opened

> **"THEY LOSE THEIR LIVES IN, LIKE, 15 MINUTES AT SOME ROCK FESTIVAL—WHICH, ALL IN ALL, IS A REALLY INSIGNIFICANT EVENT. AND IT'S THEIR ENTIRE EXISTENCE GONE!"**
> *Slash on the Castle Donington tragedy*

the concert. Although only 50,000 or so of the audience had so far entered the festival site—a vast grass slope in the middle of a motor-racing track—fans had already begun to churn the ground near the stage into thick mud.

At two o'clock on that gunmetal-grey afternoon, Duff's familiar chugging bass-riff announced their arrival and 'It's So Easy'. The weather-beaten crowd couldn't muster much of a response, though their

Axl—moody blue in a silly hat

second offering, 'Mr. Brownstone', seemed to energize the fans nearest the stage, slithering around in what proved to be lethal conditions.

In a stop-and-start set, the band attempted to calm the crowd.

"From where we were standing… it looked really hectic," reported Slash. "You couldn't tell what was happening exactly but there's a certain amount of force which goes into the first ten rows. You could see that surge when we came on, you could see the force."

The band muddled on, throwing in the new ballad 'Patience' to keep things slow and constantly berating the crowd to move back. Axl's parting shot—"have a good fuckin' day and don't kill yourselves"—turned out to be tragically prophetic. Despite the band's best efforts to defuse a confusing situation a number of fans had fallen under the tidal wave of bodies and mud. Many were carried out badly injured and the two unluckiest—20-year-old Landon Siggers and 18-year-old Alan Dick—had the life crushed out of them.

The band felt that they had done all they could, but the fact that two fans had died was a heavy burden to carry. The horror of the incident was exacerbated by unsympathetic, inaccurate reporting in the tabloid press.

COMFORTABLY NUMB

A return to the Aerosmith tour and a familiar rock'n'roll environment came as a relief for the troubled band. *The Dead Pool*, a Clint Eastwood movie they'd filmed a brief cameo appearance for, coincided with a tie-in single release for 'Welcome To The Jungle'. In the movie it was "performed" by a soon-to-be-murdered rock star and the band themselves appear briefly as mourners at his funeral. Ironically, the plot involved someone betting on who would die first out of a list of people (the dead pool), just the kind of speculation that Guns N' Roses were beginning to attract.

Appetite For Destruction was shifting copies by the million, but when the band finally came off the road they ran into a brick wall. They'd stepped on to the conveyor belt as raw-headed rockers who'd steal your drink if your back was turned. They stepped off as wealthy but bemused young men who could probably afford to buy their favourite bars.

"It was depressing, because the sense of abandon had gone," claimed Slash. "In a way we were really streetwise and hip to things, and at the same time we were really naive. That's where it screwed with us, because it totally took our innocence away." Their position as MTV favourites was beginning to grate. Slash was just getting over the

> "THE RECORD BUSINESS SUCKS. THE RECORD BUSINESS HAS TURNED MUSIC INTO A VERY UNCREATIVE, INSENSITIVE, UNMUSICAL INDUSTRY. THERE'S HARDLY ANY CHANCES BEING TAKEN ANY MORE. WE WERE A BIG CHANCE WHEN WE HAPPENED."
> *Slash*

Axl stepping out of the shadows.

notion of being able to play Aerosmith covers like 'Mama Kin' with Aerosmith, when he was faced with the idea of cover-bands playing his songs in bars.

Meanwhile, with the *Live ?!*@ Like A Suicide* EP fetching large sums from collectors, people were clamouring for a reissue. In lieu of a new album, Geffen paired it with four acoustic out-takes the band had recorded a while back. Dubbed *Guns N' Roses Lies—The Sex, The Drugs, The Violence, The Shocking Truth* (often simply called *Guns N' Roses Lies*), the December 1988 release parodied the British tabloids with its sleeve of highly improbable headlines and wry comments from the band.

Moving into 1989, 'Patience' provided the band with another success—though not before they had issued 'Paradise City' as the next major hit from *Appetite For Destruction*, complete with Donington footage on what proved to be a much-screened video. While *Guns N' Roses Lies* could hardly compete with *Appetite For Destruction* in terms of breadth of vision, the album (or EP as the band insisted on referring to it) exposed a few more of Guns N' Roses' many facets and inevitably sold by the truck-load. At one point Guns N' Roses had both *Guns N' Roses Lies* and *Appetite For Destruction* in the US top 5

> **"I ALWAYS BELIEVED THAT THE TRUTH ABOUT WHAT'S GOING ON IN GUNS N' ROSES' LIVES IS JUST AS EXCITING AND JUST AS DANGEROUS, HEAVY AND REAL AS PEOPLE THOUGHT THE HYPE SCENE TO BE."**
> *Axl*

simultaneously—the only band in 15 years to achieve such a feat. One of the acoustic tracks, 'One In A Million', took up the thread of urban terror that 'Welcome To The Jungle' had revelled in—only this time Axl was playing the scared teenager ready to bite back, rather than the gloating protagonist on 'Welcome To The Jungle'. Specifically, the song—working title 'Police And Niggers'—read like an incitement to hatred, against gays, against blacks,

against anyone "who can barely speak English" as the sleeve-notes put it. Axl seemed to miss the point that his own feelings of persecution did not give him the right to abuse his position in order to persecute others. A scandal soon erupted.

"I went back and forth from Indiana eight times, my first year in Hollywood," Axl explained. "I wrote it about being dropped off at the bus station and everything that was going on… the black guys trying to sell you drugs is where the line 'Police and niggers, get out of my way' comes from. I've seen these huge black dudes pull bowie-knives on people for their boom boxes [ghetto blasters] and shit. It's ugly… When I say I'm just a small-town white boy, I'm just saying that I'm no better than anyone else I've described. I'm just trying to get through life, that's all."

The more pressure the singer came under to recant, the more convoluted his defences became—he was doing people a favour by making them think about racism… He was using words like nigger because they were taboo… The song was merely a bad-taste joke that had lost its humour when delivered deadpan… No amount of verbal squirming could gloss over the incontrovertible fact that Axl had badly

Izzy, the quiet man who got the ball rolling.

Izzy and Axl on stage with the Stones—but Jagger wasn't always so happy.

misjudged things.

The track caused Slash considerable embarrassment, for obvious reasons. Although he went on record to say: "I don't think that statement served any good." He conceded that, "Axl has a strong feeling about it and he really wants to say it." It

seemed that, half-hearted excuses aside, Axl would not back down and his band members were expected to rally round whatever their own personal feelings.

USERS DISILLUSIONED

By the summer of 1989 the camaraderie of old had evaporated, to be replaced by a routine of detached boredom and listlessness. The hits continued to roll in, with 'Sweet Child O'Mine' being reissued in Europe

Izzy and Axl meet Stones Keith and Ronnie.

to confirm their new found popularity. But the band, now in various luxury lairs purchased with hefty royalty cheques, were too busy getting high to notice or care. They were dropped from the bill of a New York AIDS benefit concert titled 'A Rock In A Hard Place' when attention was drawn to the lyrical content

> **"AXL WAS LIKE A SERIOUS LUNATIC WHEN I MET HIM. HE WAS JUST REALLY FUCKING BENT ON FIGHTING AND DESTROYING THINGS. SOMEBODY'D LOOK AT HIM WRONG AND HE'D JUST, LIKE, START A FIGHT."**
> *Izzy*

to Los Angeles—clock up another arrest to the rap sheet. The band relocated to Chicago in an attempt to escape from the temptations of LA. Or at least Slash and the rhythm section did—Axl apparently left them to it, and Izzy had plans of his own. But the Chicago sessions came to a halt when a newspaper printed the band's location.

Izzy, meanwhile, had gone to Europe. On his blurred "grand European tour" he crossed paths with Nick Kent of fashion magazine *The Face*, in Paris. Kent took a disdainful look at the band through Izzy's rather incoherent mumblings. The questions were direct: "Are you physically addicted to hard drugs?" The answers damning: "Listen, I can't even... I

of 'One In A Million'. So they sat around and got stoned some more. Axl managed to guest on an album by former Sex Pistol Steve Jones, but seemed unable to produce one of his own.

They made a few attempts to begin a sequel to the multi-million selling *Appetite For Destruction* but achieved little. On the way to one such session, an inebriated Izzy urinated in the galley of a US Air flight

And then there were four—where's Steven?

don't... I'm OK, y'know... Everyone has to know their own limits."

Izzy's second media encounter came on a visit to the German offices of European hard rock magazine *Metal Hammer*. One spectator was music journo Chris Welch, who remembers Izzy being, "very thin and pale faced. He was standing against a wall as if he was trying to bury himself in it, trying to hide... he was very worried about people attacking him, picking fights with him in bars and the police being after him." His paranoia came over during an unscheduled interview which turned into a desperate, confused rant by Stradlin about police harassment and impending revolution. It reads like a clairvoyant insight into the later LA riots, though it probably represents no more than a reflection of Izzy's fear of all those he figured were "out ta get me".

"Things are just boilin' over," worried Stradlin. "The people are pissed off with all the shit that's going on in the States. They'll grab baseball bats and guns and will start something that will have a copycat effect all over the country. They've had enough of this bullshit."

ROSES STONED

The more copies *Appetite For Destruction* sold, the more pressure Guns N' Roses came under; the worse the pressure, the more erratic their behaviour became. The band's approach to the media firestorm seemed to be to pour more petrol on the blaze and then complain about the heat. At the American Music Awards, Slash managed to slur his way through a few four letter words by way of accepting a couple of unexpected awards. The phone lines lit up with complaints.

In a bold attempt to retain some musical focus, the band chose to accept an offer to open for the Rolling Stones towards the end of 1989—four

Teenage idol? Axl caught in pin-up pout shocker.

Axl at Farm Aid: it would be Steven's last show.

prestigious shows at the Los Angeles Coliseum. The band's performances turned out to be respectable enough, but the real sensation came when Axl used the occasion to announce his intention to leave the band unless certain members—presumably Izzy, Slash and Steven Adler—stopped "dancing with 'Mr Brownstone'".

> "WE DON'T GO OUT OF OUR WAY TO LOOK FOR TROUBLE, BUT THE SLIGHTEST INCIDENT TAKES ON UNBELIEVABLE PROPORTIONS. WE CAUSE SOME CHAOS, BECAUSE WE THINK THAT'S WHAT ROCK'N'ROLL IS ABOUT."
> *Slash*

Slash, who'd apparently relapsed into heavy heroin use after the death of his beloved grandmother, later claimed that people shouldn't credit Axl's outburst with too much influence on his decision to clean-up. But clearly the band had problems.

In addition, the notorious 'One In A Million' returned to haunt them, with guitarist Vernon Reid of all-black rock act Living Colour (who'd been guesting with the Stones throughout their tour) going out of his way to point out that: "If you don't have a problem with gay people, don't call them faggots. If you don't have a problem with black people, don't call them niggers." Axl wavered between trying to make his peace over the issue and lambasting anyone who'd dare impinge on his free speech.

The Stones got more than they bargained for—Guns N' Roses helped pack their LA shows out but stole much of their thunder, making headlines in every paper in town. Mick Jagger was furious at what he saw as attempts to upstage the headliners and issued warnings of legal action should Axl follow through on his threats to split the band before the end of the four-night Stones/Guns N' Roses run.

Meanwhile, Vince Neil of Motley Crüe seemed

Steven—too party hardy for his own good

Matt Sorum, taking a break from pulling the band together

determined to win some kudos and publicity by escalating a simmering feud with Guns N' Roses which dated back to Vince punching Izzy for flirting with his wife (others claimed that Vince's wife had concocted the story after her attempts to pick up Izzy had been rebuffed). Since he took any assault on Guns N' Roses personally, Axl had been trading insults with Vince in the press—1989 lurched into 1990 with business as usual…

ADLER OUT, DIZZY IN

The spring of 1990 brought major personnel changes for the band. In came Dizzy Reed, a down-on-his-luck piano player who'd once rehearsed in the next studio to the infant Guns N' Roses and even, apparently, been asked to join the band, whereupon he promptly injured his hand in a car crash. The way Dizzy tells it: "Having a keyboard player in the band was something they talked about a long time ago. I never really thought it would happen."

However, on the verge of being evicted from his apartment, the penniless muso made a fateful call to Axl.

"I go, 'Dude, I'm starving, as of tomorrow I'll have no

phone, no apartment, no food, no nothing, and if you guys need to know where to get a hold of me, I can't tell you where I'm gonna be'."

Axl picked up the story: "I found out he was going to be put out on the streets… So I call Alan (Niven) on Monday and I say, 'secure this guy, hire him, write up the contracts. Put him on a salary and give him an advance so he can get an apartment'."

The other line-up news would involve an exit, not an entrance. But first the band managed to piece together one track—the brooding, ambitious 'Civil War'—and donate it to a charity album, *Nobody's Angel*, compiled

Matt Sorum, with the Cult—but not for long

> **"I PERSONALLY LOVE OUR SONGS. THE BOTTOM LINE IS THIS, IF THIS WERE ALL TO FINISH TOMORROW THEN AT LEAST I'VE GOT 'EM ON TAPE. I'M NOT WRITING THIS FOR YOU, I'M NOT WRITING THIS FOR ANYBODY WHO LISTENS TO IT. I'M DOING IT FOR ME."**
> *Axl*

A shorter-lived union was Axl's long-threatened wedding to Erin Everly which lasted all of 48 hours before Everly, with a temper that allegedly matched Axl's, demanded that the marriage be annulled. Back with the band, Slash and Izzy had managed to overcome their drug problems, but Stevie, the happy-go-lucky junkie, couldn't grasp that hard drugs and rock'n'roll were no longer considered a winning combination. Adler had been demoted from full membership and placed on a salary in an attempt to force him to face up to the severity of the situation. Duff made personal threats to Adler's drug dealer to leave the hapless drummer alone. But the band finally decided that Adler had to go.

"The misconception is that we kicked him out for the hell of it and that I was the dictator behind it," claimed Axl. "The truth is, I probably fought a little harder to keep him in the band, because I wasn't working with him on a daily basis like the other guys were. They grew tired of not being able to get their work done because Steven wasn't capable…" However, Axl did resent the fact that Adler had been assigned a share of the band's songwriting royalties and that "he's been able to live off of that money, buy a shitload of drugs and hire lawyers to sue me… He's a real damaged person, but

by ex-Beatle George Harrison and his wife Olivia. This new song was debuted at Farm Aid, the annual American agricultural workers' benefit concert, where the band (minus new-boy Reed) also performed 'Welcome To The Jungle' and 'Down On The Farm'—an obscure cover of one of Duff's fave punk outfits, the UK Subs. It would be Steven Adler's final major assignment with the band.

Slash takes it easy for once.

> **"WHEN WE GET UP IN THE AFTERNOON TO DO A SOUNDCHECK, WE DRINK SO MUCH THAT WE CAN'T PLAY, BECAUSE OUR HANDS ARE SHAKING LIKE WINDMILLS. SO WHAT HAPPENS? WE DRINK... AND THEN WE'RE FINE, AND WE WAKE UP THE NEXT DAY WITH SOME FLOOZIE... YOU DON'T KNOW HER NAME..."**
> *Slash*

Adam Marples of the Sea Hags; then Martin Chambers of the Pretenders recorded demos with the band, but he wasn't considered "over-the-top like we needed", according to Duff. Salvation finally came in the shape of burly Californian Matt Sorum, a one time session-player who'd worked with Guns N' Roses associates the Cult. While Duff claimed that he'd "never, ever want to hurt another band" he admitted that when he and Slash saw their old compadres play at the Universal Amphitheatre in LA, he couldn't help but hope that the Cult's ever-changing line-up would soon send the drummer into the open arms of Guns N' Roses.

Though Matt's ultra-powerful poundings lacked a little of Adler's fast and loose Hollywood shuffle (even Slash was forced to concede that "some of the immediacy of our sound was lost in losing Steven; it almost had a touch of anxiety to it"), Sorum's steadying hand helped pull the band together—Slash has also said that without Sorum the band might have disintegrated completely.

Instead, they quickly began pumping out track after track as the recording sessions finally went up a gear.

"I heard a lot of stories before I joined, so I knew they were in chaos," joked Sorum. "I'd heard the rumours about Steven. I just didn't think I'd be the guy they'd call in to save them, or whatever!" His fears about "walking into an opium den" were unfounded. The band

he's making choices to keep himself damaged."

MEET MATT

Having amputated Adler, they discovered that replacing him was not going to be easy. They contemplated

powered into intense and protracted recording, with Mick Clink at the production desk. Guns N' Roses wanted to get as much material as possible down on tape—in case such an opportunity never occurred again.

Release dates were regularly set, then scrapped. The album was eventually rumoured to be a double album, or maybe two single albums with the second being released half way through the inevitable tour. Or even two full-length CDs (both double-records in vinyl format) to be released simultaneously. Then there was

> **"I DID A ROLLING STONE PIECE. I SAID IN THE ARTICLE THERE WERE THREE THINGS I DIDN'T WANT TO TALK ABOUT: AXL, MY DRUGS PAST, AND OTHER BANDS. SO WHEN IT COMES OUT, THE FIRST THING IT SAYS IS: 'SLASH ON AXL ROSE AND DRUGS'."**
>
> *Slash*

Lenny Kravitz, a collaborator with both Slash and Duff

talk of a series of themed EPs—a rap EP, a punk EP and so on.

Said Duff: "Most bands—whatever happens to them—once a year they go on tour, make another record, go on tour. We're not like that… we're not a business. We do walk our own path. But, you know, most important—music is something that cannot be explained. It comes from your heart… and if you feel like doing all this music, if it takes all this time and all that stuff, then so be it… So I apologize to the kids for taking so long. But I think… I hope that a lot of them understood where we're coming from. Everybody put their heart and soul into it and that's what matters."

Meanwhile Slash even found time to play on Michael Jackson's *Dangerous* album, though all his work was done without the presence of the enigmatic star. He also played and wrote with Lenny Kravitz for his *Mama Said…* album (both had attended the same high school, though not at the same time), laid down a solo on Alice Cooper's *Hey Stoopid* album, failed to impress Bob Dylan in the studio (the feeling was mutual), turned down sessions with David Bowie's Tin Machine, but played alongside Duff on Iggy Pop's *Brick By Brick* album. Phew!

MOST GROUPS ARE HAPPY TO DO AS THEY'RE TOLD IN ORDER TO SUCCEED AND BE COMMERCIAL, EVEN GIVE UP THEIR IDENTITY. WE NEVER WANTED TO DO THAT. THAT'S WHY WE'RE THE NEW PUBLIC ENEMY NUMBER ONE, AND EVERY SHERIFF AND COP WANTS JUST ONE THING, TO NAIL GUNS N' ROSES
Slash

Bob Dylan, the 'Knocking On Heaven's Door' man

BACK IN BLACK

Welcome to 1991. The band drafted in Bill Price (who had co-produced the Sex Pistols' *Never Mind The Bollocks*) to remix the sessions, delaying matters even further. The last public airing of new material had been a rough version of Bob Dylan's classic 'Knocking On Heaven's Door', which had appeared many months before, on the soundtrack of the Tom Cruise movie *Days Of Thunder*.

Secrecy surrounded the ever-expanding *Use Your Illusion I & II* (the title came from a Mark Kostabi painting chosen by Axl—carrying on in the tradition of *Appetite For Destruction*, though lacking a little in impact). But surprisingly, the band began the new year with a pair of concerts as part of the 'Rock In Rio II' festival in Brazil.

The Guns N' Roses that arrived in Rio were clearly changed men and not just because of the presence of Dizzy and Matt. They isolated themselves from the other rock acts at the four-day festival, surrounding themselves with intimidating bodyguards

Rock In Rio—the band blast back.

Axl, bare-chested in Brazil

and snubbing old associates. They also refused to co-operate with the media, which only made the press more determined to print any scraps of information they could gather. Moreover, they would only be photographed by a handful of trusted acquaintances. When they did permit an interview, they insisted on a contract that would give the band complete approval over the contents and where it could, or could not, be

Slash shines at sunset.

published—with default resulting in a punitive $200,000 (£130,000) law suit. Most refused to sign— one US music magazine simply printed the contract in an attempt to embarrass the group.

"As soon as the band started to become popular there were all these people taking unnecessary pot shots at us," reasoned Slash. "So we thought, 'Fuck it!'."

Both Matt and Dizzy were thrown in at the deep end—though they'd rehearsed with the rest of the band, the first time they'd played in a live situation with Axl was in front of 125,000 people. The combination of local hysteria at the presence of these demi-gods of rock and quiet bemusement at the new material they were showcasing made for confusing shows—Axl was frustrated by the lack of audience response as the band felt their way through newies like 'Pretty Tied Up', 'Double Talkin' Jive' and the lengthy epic 'Estranged'.

Dizzy and Matt were hanging on for dear life— neither possessed a set list (Axl chose the running order on the spot) and Matt was expected to supply a drum solo at short notice, despite never having played one before. But even with these hitches, Axl deemed the new line-up to be a success.

> **"WE LIKE TO EXPRESS OUR FRUSTRATIONS WITH LIFE THROUGH OUR MUSIC. INSTEAD OF GETTING INTO A FIGHT WE PUT IT INTO OUR MUSIC. THAT'S WHY I LIKE TO PLAY AS MUCH AS POSSIBLE, BECAUSE IT KEEPS US MUCH CALMER AND WE CAN DEAL WITH PEOPLE BETTER THAT WAY..."**
> *Axl*

BACK ON THE ROAD AGAIN

With the band scheduled to start touring soon, work continued on the *Use Your Illusion I & II* sessions. Axl decided that in order for the record to be finished, the band would have to sack manager Alan Niven. While not all shared his views, the Axl-ization of the band

was well and truly under way.

With Niven's junior partner Doug Goldstein now installed as manager (but Axl very much in the driving seat) the band played a trio of low-key club dates in San Francisco, LA and New York—'public rehearsals' for an abundance of new songs. In fact, to help him cope with the amount of new material, Axl had his lyrics fed to him on stage by teleprompter. Then he managed to injure his foot at the Ritz in New York, stage-diving into the crowd—so he began gigging in late May with his left foot in a bizarre cast, apparently created by sports-shoe designers.

The tour—confrontationally dubbed 'Get In The Ring'—got underway in May, even though the *Use Your Illusion I & II* records were nowhere to be seen. But by now, no one expected Guns N' Roses to follow any sort of familiar, music-industry logic. The first serious incidents occurred at a gig in in St Louis' Riverport Performing Arts Centre, where conflict between Axl, local security guards and a local motorcycle gang escalated into a riot. Axl had instructed security to remove a camera that one of the local bikers had been flaunting. When they did nothing, Axl took it upon himself to tackle the front-row fan and a scuffle broke out. Rose (who lost a contact lens in the scrum) announced that "thanks to lame-ass security, I'm going home" and walked off—

> "WE NEVER HAD ANY MONEY AND THAT'S PROBABLY WHY WE DIDN'T KILL OURSELVES BACK THEN... I REMEMBER AXL AND I ONCE VOLUNTEERED AS MEDICAL TEST SUBJECTS FOR UCLA THINKING WE'D GET PILLS OR SOMETHING. BUT IT WAS JUST A SMOKING TEST AND ALL WE GOT WAS SOME FREE CIGARETTES."
> ***Slash***

90 minutes into the show. Feeling short changed, the crowd became increasingly restless. Rose later claimed that the band decided to return in an attempt to restore order. But by then a fully-fledged riot had begun. Guns N' Roses resisted the notion that they were responsible for inciting a riot which caused thousands of dollars worth of damages. Although they'd been playing lengthy sets on the tour, they were only contractually obliged to play an hour and a half—which they had—and a clause in their contract exempted them from any damage caused to a venue where alcohol was on sale—as had been the case. But a warrant was issued for Axl's arrest on charges of "assault" and "inciting a riot", though he was already out of the jurisdiction of Missouri State before it could be served.

OPENING SHOT

The band had initially planned to release the maudlin 'Don't Cry' as the first single from *Use Your Illusion I & II*, but then wisely opted for the harder opening volley of the snarling 'You Could Be Mine'. The track tied-in with the new Arnold Schwarzenegger blockbuster, *Terminator 2*, though Guns N' Roses hardly needed the extra promotional push. This was as much an advert for Arnie's new movie and Arnie even made the effort to appear in their video—more than could be said for Izzy…

While the band travelled on the plush, chartered MGM jet, the guitarist drove from gig to gig on his own tour bus, to help him retain some grip on reality. It

A moody moment from Axl

also kept him away from the rest of the band, and Axl in particular. The singer had developed a nasty habit of keeping crowds waiting long after the advertised start-time at gigs. He'd place the blame on hassle from Geffen Records, or crucial work with his therapist, or even his masseur. But late starts often meant late finishes and hefty fines from local venues or unions who operated a curfew. Izzy felt that this could be avoided if only Axl would demonstrate a little consideration for fans and band alike.

The band continued to power their way across America, the cloud of the St Louis riot hanging over them and Axl ranting from the stage whenever the notion took him. The first American leg of the tour climaxed on August 3, with a mammoth three hours and 20 minutes of Guns N' Roses histrionics at the Los Angeles Forum, on the final night of a four-show residency.

RETURN OF THE CREW?

In exile, Steven Adler attempted to resurrect the Road Crew name with San Franciscan frontman Davy Vain. But as the group was basically Vain's previous band now calling themselves the Road Crew, the set up

Spotlight kids Axl and Duff get down to some rocking.

was less Adler's creation than a kind of ready-made half-way house.

"I've never played with a drummer before who is so identifiably himself," gushed Vain. "He can play one of our new tunes and it'll remind me of something Guns N' Roses did... It's his build-ups, his cowbell and his kick-drum patterns... everything's more groovy and bouncy." The new Road Crew enjoyed a brief flurry of attention from a rock press hungry for any Guns N' Roses-related story. But Adler had

CHAPTER 5: BACK IN BLACK

apparently not put his problems as far behind him as he'd thought. As a result Road Crew slipped quietly off the agenda.

Axl keeps yet another crowd in the palm of his hand.

GET INTO EUROPE

Guns N' Roses' next stop was Europe, for a month of dates. With their usual panache, they managed to blow out one show in Norway and then stage one of their infamous tantrums to disrupt an already late-running show in Mannheim, Germany—picking up a whopping fine in the process. Their European visit ended at London's Wembley Arena, on August 31, 1991.

Support act Skid Row entertained the masses

Right: Axl stops running for a moment or two.

with hard rock-riffing and foul profanities (earning themselves a ban from the local council, for daring to perform their anthem 'Get The Fuck Out'). But Axl's specially-invited guests, electro-rock industrialists Nine Inch Nails, simply left the fans baffled rather than amused. Then, after the now traditional extended interval, Guns N' Roses returned to lay siege to the city where they'd played their first overseas gigs—four years previously. It was to be Izzy Stradlin's final show with the band.

Their stage show had developed in fits and starts. Axl remained in perpetual motion, covering every inch of the stage on a marathon run interrupted only to accommodate slower mood pieces like 'November Rain', and a number of occasionally ludicrous costume changes—cycling shorts, t-shirts, an assortment of garish jackets and even tartan kilts. At Wembley, the crowd's unfamiliarity with unreleased songs from *Use Your Illusion I & II* (including 'Bad Obsession' and an elaborate 'Estranged' delivered as a crowd-cooling encore), took some of the wind out of Guns N' Roses' impact. Axl, however, was too busy

Left: An increasingly unhappy Izzy

Izzy's new band of men—the Ju Ju Hounds

baiting the press to notice, baring his ass to demonstrate his contempt of *Kerrang!*—who'd championed the band in the early days.

CHOKE ON THIS

Use Your Illusion I & II emerged, in a fanfare of late night record store openings, at midnight on September 16, 1991. The floodgates had opened, and over 140 minutes of new Guns N' Roses music poured down upon the fans like manna from heaven (or perhaps it's more true to the spirit of the band to say it came like thunder from hell).

But was this quantity instead of quality? Slash implied that anyone unable to swallow it all at once (or simply lacking the funds) should buy one and tape the other from a friend. Few took them up on this apparently generous suggestion, most buying the pair simultaneously, sending both albums charging to the top of the charts (with *Use Your Illusion II* nudging slightly ahead to score the Number 1 slot).

For their money, fans got not just the newest

Slash coping with the trials of being a guitar sex god—it's hard

Guns N' Roses tunes, but some of the oldest as well. Slash : "We wanted to do some of the songs we couldn't do on the first album because of time and finances. We wanted to clear the slate so that on the next album we could start afresh."

Tracks held back in reserve included the brutally misogynistic 'Back Off Bitch' which, in light of previous hassles, you'd think Axl might have wanted to leave gathering dust in the attic. But the singer felt it important to get these kind of things out into the open—"We do a certain song because we want to express that anger… 'We did it. OK—now I can deal with the person that I just called an asshole.' That's healthy."

A STAB OF DOOM

One of the great unsung heroes of *Use Your Illusion I & II* is Axl's bold psychodrama 'Coma', their doomiest heavy-metal excursion yet. It shared a sense of gonzoid concept-album theatricality with the spooky Alice Cooper duet 'The Garden' and Izzy apparently found it nearly impossible to play live. But it beats tracks like 'Right Next Door To Hell', the generic opening rocker on *Use Your Illusion I* which attempted—and failed—to recapture the short-fuse mentality of the rawer cuts on *Appetite For Destruction*.

"Writing 'Coma' was so heavy I'd start to write and I'd just pass out," explained Axl. "I tried to write that song for a year… I wrote the whole end of that song off the top of my head. It just poured out…" There was a huge range of material to choose from on the albums, and although everyone has a different favourite, Guns N' Roses seemed at their best on *Use Your Illusion I & II*'s everything-including-the-kitchen-sink blow outs. 'November Rain', Axl's much talked about masterpiece, lived up to that hype with crashing strings, a spine-chilling atmosphere and a soaring guitar solo.

Duff took a stab at vocals for the pleasingly gruff 'So Fine', while Izzy knocked out shuffling rockers that seemed homesick for the bar-rooms the band no longer played. Slash peppered the album with lethal soloing. Axl added a less-than-rivetting semi-rap electronic track 'My World' that Izzy only found out about when he saw it on the record. Covers of Dylan's 'Knocking On Heaven's Door' and Paul McCartney's 'Live And Let Die' seemed laboured—on the former, Axl's vocals are mannered to the point of self parody, while the latter indicates that no one in the band had the guts to tell Axl when an idea stank.

They had also roped in some old buddies, including Michael Monroe of Hanoi Rocks fame, who added some saxophone, and even Axl's brother Stewart, who got a shot at backing vocals. The press weren't forgotten—considered worthy of a mention

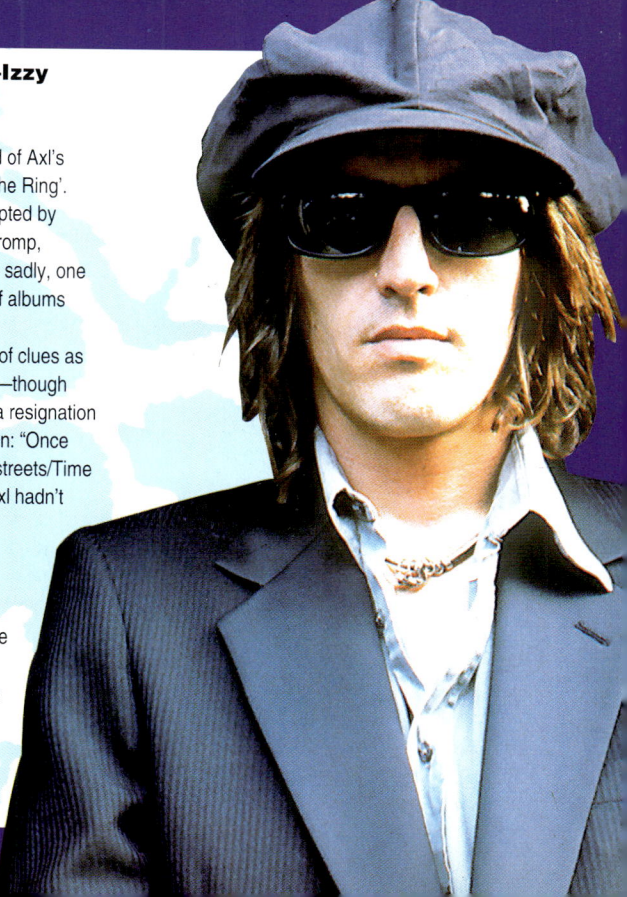

Mean, moody Ju Ju Hound—Izzy Stradlin

were various journalists at the receiving end of Axl's wrath (and some free publicity) on 'Get In The Ring'. This was originally a Duff composition, co-opted by Axl—who'd turned it into a rum pantomime romp, complete with boxing-ring sound effects. So sadly, one of the better full-on rock tracks on the pair of albums was squandered on a ludicrous rant.

The records' lyric sheets provide plenty of clues as to the band's state of mind. 'Pretty Tied Up'—though superficially a tale of kinky sex—is virtually a resignation letter from the song's composer, Izzy Stradlin: "Once there was this rock'n'roll band rollin' on the streets/Time went by and it became a joke…". Strange Axl hadn't noticed when he sang it.

IZZY OUT?

Appetite For Destruction had credited all songs collectively to Guns N' Roses (with the occasional co-write shared with Axl's buddy West Arkeen, or Hollywood Rose man Chris Weber). But on *Use Your Illusion I & II* , the credits were more specific—presumably to ensure that no one stole any of Axl's compositional glory on tracks like

Gilby Clarke, the guy who got the job when Izzy departed.

'November Rain'. This revealed that Izzy had clocked up more songwriting credits (12 individual or co-written tracks) over *Use Your Illusion I & II*'s 30 tracks, than Slash (with a mere nine). He'd even started to handle a few lead vocals, both on record and live. Despite growing alienation, the man responsible for much of the original Guns N' Roses concept was quietly making his presence felt.

But Izzy's frustration with Axl finally boiled over. He had refused to take part in the singer's expensive concept video for 'Don't Cry', calling it a waste of money and only days after the release of *Use Your Illusion I & II*, with the band on a break between tours, Izzy turned his back on the Guns N' Roses empire. After much speculation, his departure was made official in November.

A bitter Axl claimed: "Izzy wanted the financial rewards and power rewards of my vision. Izzy's vision was much smaller." Despite Izzy's many songwriting credits, Rose hinted that, "in order to make certain things happen, certain people had to think certain ideas were completely their own."

Axl further claimed that Izzy had no interest in making proper recordings of his rough demos. "Izzy's songs were on the record because I wanted them on the record," he raged, "not because Izzy gave a shit either way." He even declared that Izzy's live

Gilby and Dizzy, the new kids on the block

performances represented poor value for money because he didn't run around enough on stage!

Despite all of this, Rose claimed that people didn't appreciate "how painful that experience was… when I got the phone call that Izzy was leaving the band I was standing there crying… my friend of 15 years was leaving".

EVERY DOG HAS HIS DAY

Stradlin bounced back relatively quickly. Having once fled Indiana, he was now just as happy to quit LA.

"I didn't touch a guitar for a couple of months," he explained. "I just took up where I left off on my motor-trials riding… then when it was cold I was forced back indoors.

"Being in Guns N' Roses, it would be kind of hard to just put an ad in a paper sayin' 'Izzy looking for band'. It would be crazy…" But forming an alliance with ex-Broken Homes bassist Jimmy Ashhurst got him back on track: "Jimmy's got phone numbers on every rock musician goin'." Naming his new band after "some old Alice Cooper song called 'Black Ju Ju'" he teamed up with ex-Georgia Satellites guitarist Rick Richards and drummer Charlie Quintana, then

Slash makes Gilby feel at home.

rattled off an album in double quick time.

Izzy Stradlin and the Ju Ju Hounds rode a fairly straightforward, unfussy groove, comparable with Rolling Stone Keith Richard's rootsy solo albums. In fact, Keith's old Stones crony, Ronnie Wood, made an appearance on 'Take A Look At The Guy', a cover from one of Wood's own solo LPs. Izzy soon set out on an extensive club tour of Europe and the US, but fans expecting to hear Guns N' Roses favourites were disappointed—the only covers he seemed interested in were old rock'n'roll tunes.

CALL GILBY FOR THRILLS

Gilby Clarke, a veteran of poppy LA scenesters Candy and the sleazier Kill For Thrills, became the latest Guns N' Roses recruit. The band initially courted Jane's Addiction guitarist Dave Navarro, a fairly esoteric choice. But Clarke, sporting an Aerosmithy mop of dark hair (and scarves and bangles accessories), looked like an appropriate choice. He was given a typical Guns N' Roses baptism of fire.

"Literally from the day I walked in it was three weeks to the first show. A lot of people, like the fans, didn't know, it was so quick. I'd be out there playing

> **"THE DIFFERENCES OF OPINION WERE BETWEEN ME AND AXL. I TRIED TO RESOLVE THE PROBLEMS WITH HIM BEFORE I LEFT, BUT IT DIDN'T LOOK TOO PROMISING."**
> *Izzy*

and I think some people were looking at me like, 'Go, Izzy, go!', 'cos we kinda look the same.

"I knew it was working but I didn't think it was really gonna happen. It didn't sink in until the first show… I had known Matt Sorum for quite a long time. Duff and Slash I hadn't really known, but I'd run into them over the years. It was comfortable to go down with at least Matt on my side. But this is what I'd been dreaming of all those years. To get thrown into it was like an unbelievable pay-off after 10 years of playing."

HEROICS AND HORRORS

As well as the new guy, there were new girls and even a second keyboard player to confuse the fans when the band set out for the second bout of American touring, at the beginning of December, 1991. Two female backing singers, three female horn players and portly harmonica/keyboard player Teddy Andreadis brought the on-stage head-count to 12. Minus Izzy, the band forged on with further late-starts, run-ins with the media, and at least one Axl outburst—in Ohio, where Axl rejected the notion suggested in the press that Guns N' Roses would be the perfect house band for budding right-wing politician, and ex-Ku Klux Klan member, David Duke. The dark cloud of St Louis re-emerged in Chicago, where local sheriffs threatened to extradite Axl to St Louis, where he was still a wanted man.

The touring continued across America until the band decamped to Europe in April to play the Freddie Mercury tribute show. The gig itself went well, but Axl was reported as being more distant than usual from his band mates, choosing to party with Liza Minnelli instead and perhaps feeling, in such exalted company, that he'd outgrown Guns N' Roses (some would say that he seemed hell bent, by this point, on turning Guns N' Roses into a solo project). But in secret meetings it was still all go for the group. They inked a deal to tour America with the only other rock band who could compare with them in terms of

> "EVERYTHING ABOUT [AXL] AS A PERFORMER AND A SINGER COMES FROM HIS PERSONALITY, SO THE SHIT THAT MAKES HIM CRAZY OR THE SHIT THAT HE FINDS HARD TO DEAL WITH IS, AT THE SAME TIME, WHAT MAKES HIS TALENT."
> *Slash*

stature—Metallica.

When Axl arrived late at Heathrow Airport for the flight home, the security guards refused to search his baggage by hand, rather than expose his collection of homeopathic medicines to an X-Ray scan, and so he threw his standard tantrum. Life went on…

After returning to the States to announce the impending Guns N' Roses/Metallica mega-tour, the band set out on their biggest European tour so far. The opening night, Saturday May 16, at Slaine Castle near Dublin, Eire, had local worthies fuming at the prospect of young colleens baring their breasts for the crowd's pre-show entertainment on giant video screens—a rather puerile trend the band had encouraged, which involved unfair abuse piled on anyone picked out by the video cameras who didn't want to go along with the 'fun'. But the band seemed impressed by the Irish crowd's antics, Slash declaring that "I can always tell a drinking town when the people in the bar get drunk before me".

The band went on to entertain the "ex-Commie bastards" (as they put it) of Czechoslovakia, before taking in Vienna, Berlin, Stuttgart, Hannover and Paris—where they broadcast live on assorted television networks. Though a proposed on-stage jam with Jeff Beck had to be cancelled, the presence of Lenny Kravitz and Aerosmith's Tyler and Perry more

Axl gives it all he's got—

Manchester, England, with Rose either exhausted, or hung-over and sulking following his blast at Beatty— depending on who you believed. They did, however, reprise renditions of Queen's 'Tie Your Mother Down' and 'We Will Rock You' when Brian May turned up to play with them at Wembley in London.

And on they trundled—pausing only for Axl to be shaken-down by British customs again. After Switzerland, the Netherlands and Italy, Slash took

...and again—

than compensated for this. Rose was typically reticent on revelations that his current love, model Stephanie Seymour, had been spotted stepping-out with actor Warren Beatty. Axl flew into a tirade, dedicating "Double Talking Jive' to the actor he called "a parasite who likes to play games with people's lives".

The band cancelled their next show, to be held in

part in Michael Jackson's 'Give In To Me' video shoot. Then came Spain, where due to venue problems, the band were reluctantly forced to cancel.

DAMAGE INC.

Having put a mostly crisis-free Euro-tour behind them, and with 'November Rain' released in the US as a suitably lavish single ("It's funny, because I always thought music was indulgent in the first place", laughed Slash), Axl returned to America where he was arrested at New York's JFK airport—the St Louis riot warrant had finally caught up with him. But with a trial deferred to October (resulting in an eventual $50,000–£35,700 fine), Guns N' Roses squared off for a tour with Metallica, a move which created the hottest ticket of the summer in the US and lined the two bands up for inevitable comparisons.

While Guns N' Roses were the bigger band over-all and were nominally headlining the equal-billings shows, Metallica were doing slightly better business with their leaner, eponymous single album. Metallica were also carrying less dead-weight live and, bloated by their ever-expanding entourage, Guns N' Roses seemed to be suffering. Metallica wisely realized that playing last meant playing to an energy-drained

Axl—does the sun shine out of his behind?

crowd. Axl, meanwhile, was in an increasingly ego-driven state, and seemed to take the fact that Nirvana had declined to take the opening slot on tour as a personal slight. And despite a united public front, rivalry between Guns N' Roses and Metallica was festering. First, three shows were blown out when Axl

> "EVERYTHING IS PIECED TOGETHER WITH SAMPLES... WHICH IS SO DIFFERENT TO WHAT WE DO. MICHAEL HIRES OUT THE STUDIO FOR, LIKE, 10 YEARS AND SHOWS UP ONCE A MONTH. I'LL PROBABLY NEVER GET TO MEET HIM."
> *Slash on Michael Jackson*

was ordered to rest his voice for a week. Then, on the fateful night of August 8, in Montreal, Metallica's James Hetfield was badly burned in a pyrotechnics accident. Axl cut short the Guns N' Roses set the same night, blaming sound problems and causing a minor riot in the process.

Though more shows were cancelled, Hetfield made a remarkable recovery and Metallica didn't fail to compare their own resilience with Guns N' Roses' ever more haphazard behaviour. Metallica included footage of Hetfield sarcastically reading out Guns N' Roses' enormous rider (dressing-room requirements) in a home video and, as Slash put it: "it turned into such a conflict of interests between the two bands that we're no longer friends any more."

SOUTH OF THE BORDER...

As if looking for trouble, after a short break Guns N' Roses set the controls for the heart of South America. They left their first port of call, Venezuela (and much of their equipment), only hours before a military coup. In Columbia, before a delayed concert was to start, six tons of stage roof collapsed. In Chile, local police scoured the band's hotel suites in a wild goose-chase for drugs. In Brazil, rain stopped play.

Duff in a mellower moment

A month later in Japan, the band recorded footage at the Tokyo Dome to feature on two concert videos (they would also release a pair of documentary videos chronicling the making of the 'Don't Cry' and 'November Rain' videos respectively). Next stop—the largest concert ever staged in Australia.

IZZY STRADLIN—SLIGHT RETURN

Guns N' Roses seemed to have reached a point where they had nothing left to shock us with. Having dropped the backing singers and horns, returned to a core unit of six and introduced an acoustic set to their show, they dubbed the latest bunch of dates the 'Skin And Bones' tour. Despite some cancellations forced by bad weather, and one in Atlanta, Georgia, forced by previous run-ins with local law enforcement, Guns N' Roses got on with mopping up any remaining interest in *Use Your Illusion I & II*.

Then they threw a curve-ball that took everyone by surprise. Izzy Stradlin was coming back in the band—for a few European live dates, at least. Stradlin's replacement Gilby had injured his left wrist practising for a celebrity charity motorbike race. Stradlin was reputedly offered a hefty pay cheque to rescue the threatened dates, but described his brief reunion as no more than an opportunity to visit new

Country cousins? Tom Petty and Axl harmonise.

countries like Greece and Israel. No full-time position had been discussed, nor would it hold any attraction for him.

"Going back into the band was a strange and uncomfortable experience…" said Izzy. "It made me realize why I was glad to get out in the first place. It's the same old story with Axl. When he wants

> "WE'RE NOT THE EASIEST PEOPLE TO WORK WITH AND WE'VE BASICALLY GOT THIS 'SCREW YOU' ATTITUDE THAT GIVES A LOT OF PEOPLE CAUSE TO WORRY. BUT WE DO KNOW OUR LIMITS. WE STOP IF WE THINK WHAT WE'RE DOING IS GOING TO SCREW UP OUR MUSIC."
> *Axl*

something from you he's on the phone being nice and friendly. As soon as your usefulness runs out he turns on you… right after I'd done those dates he was back in the media putting me down.

"The band's egos are way out of control," Izzy reflected. "There's a feeling of unreality about them.

Duff—portrait of a rock star

Cat-scratch fever as Slash scratches his back.

Uncle Slash wants you!

"WE'RE TURNING PEOPLE ON TO SOMETHING THAT NOBODY ELSE WOULD. SO WHEN WE DO GET THIS BIG. WE CAN'T BE PISSED OFF ABOUT IT. YOU CAN'T JUST GO 'FUCK, WE'RE NOT JUST ASSHOLE PUNK ROCKERS ANY MORE'. IT SEEMS POINTLESS TO MAKE A FUSS LIKE THAT. LIKE, NIRVANA'S BEEN DOING THAT, LIKE IT'S NOT COOL ANYMORE. HEY, KEEP YOUR MUSIC END UP, THE REST GOES WITH THE TERRITORY."
Slash

Axl in rare smiling shot sensation.

They lead isolated lives and don't seem to be in touch anymore with the real world."

Happy to see that he hadn't suddenly become a 'where are they now?' trivia question as many had predicted, Gilby was reinstated as soon as he'd recovered and even appeared alongside Izzy adding backing vocals to the Guns N' Roses second night at Milton Keynes Bowl, in England—where they were also joined by Izzy's Stones buddy, Ronnie Wood, and Michael Monroe of the ever-influential Hanoi Rocks.

Guns N' Roses plodded on for a further two months hitting both new and familiar European territories, this time with virtually no incidents. The touring, which had begun with the first warm up date on Friday May 1, 1991, finally ground to a halt on Saturday, July 18, with another visit to South America, another tussle between Axl and South American police in search of drugs, and another massive concert—in front of 70,000 Brazilians at the River Plate Stadium in Buenos Aires.

SPAGHETTI AND MEATHEADS

In September Steven Adler's legal case against the band finally reached a climax. Adler had received a one-off payment in return for relinquishing any future claims on Guns N' Roses. Now he was insisting that the band were to blame for his drug addiction. This mutated into a law-suit alleging that he was entitled to a share in the value of the name Guns N' Roses, and that he'd been deceived as to the true financial worth of the band when he signed away his membership. When a judge decided that the only way to put a price on the true value of the name Guns N' Roses was to hold a public auction for the trademark, the band pressed for a quick settlement. Adler collected $2.3 (£1.5) million from the band, $50,000 ($33,000) from

> **"EVERYBODY'S INTELLECTUALIZING GUNS N' ROSES, BUT SHORT OF SOME OF AXL'S LYRICS AND SOME OF THE MUSICIANSHIP THERE'S NOTHING TO ANALYZE."**
> *Slash*

> **"I FEEL SORRY FOR HIM, BECAUSE HE DIDN'T GET ANY OF THE MONEY WE PAID HIM. IT ALL WENT TO THE PEOPLE THAT MADE HIM DO THIS. HE'S STILL ON JUNK [HEROIN] AND I STILL LOVE HIM, BUT HE'S GONNA DIE. IT'S JUST A SAD FUCKING STATE OF AFFAIRS."**
> *Duff on Steven Adler*

A boy from the wrong side of the tracks?

days in Guns N' Roses to sue the very people who saved his life…."

The band issued their own statement, saying, "we're not thrilled about having to pay more money than we are already paying him. And we continue to believe in the defence we have asserted in the law suit. But we are certainly glad to have this dispute behind us." Since Adler had had to admit under oath that he was still hooked on narcotics, the band implied that pressure from lawyers and Adler's mother were behind his decision to sue his ex-band mates.

"He ain't gettin' shit of the money that they sued for," spat Duff. "He's only getting like a 25th of it."

NOBODY LOVES ME

Meanwhile, Duff had returned to LA to find that people "didn't want me for me; they wanted me because I was this guy in Guns N' Roses". Disillusioned, he retreated to the eight-track studio in his well-appointed home to sift through the tapes he'd recorded for his own amusement during the tour promoting *Use Your Illusion I & II*. Duff seemed particularly prone to wear and tear on the road—few could have missed how bloated on beer he looked as

manager Goldstein and $150,000 (£100,000) from former manager Niven.

"I consider it insane that Steven Adler should have his junkiedom rewarded," fumed Niven. "There is something fundamentally wrong with a situation in which a junkie, expelled from the band before he could destroy both it and himself, hands over to lawyers the money he apparently retained from his

Metallica: one half of the dream-team tour that went sour.

the seemingly endless touring took its toll. But no sooner had he come off the road with Guns N' Roses than he was announcing his new pride and joy, a solo album called *Believe In Me*. Duff performed the bulk of the album himself, with buddies like Lenny Kravitz and Sebastian Bach of Skid Row filling in the gaps.

"I financed it myself," proclaimed Duff. "I wasn't even planning on doing a record, I just needed a release; I needed to get it out. That sounds like a

> **"I PRETTY MUCH FOLLOW MY OWN INTERNAL CLOCK, AND I PERFORM BETTER LATER AT NIGHT. NOTHING SEEMS TO WORK OUT FOR ME UNTIL LATER AT NIGHT."**
> *Axl*

cliché… but it was really true in my case."

His enthusiasm took him out on tour, headlining clubs in the UK and supporting hoary old rock dinosaurs the Scorpions through Europe. He also proved to be the driving force behind a new Guns N' Roses project, an expanded, so-called 'punk EP'—now an album called *The Spaghetti Incident?* The name came from an anecdote about spaghetti-leftovers stolen during a time when Adler, Slash and Duff shared an apartment in Chicago, which Adler's lawyers solemnly referred to as "the spaghetti incident" whenever this was mentioned in court.

Get in the ring!

There's no stopping Slash.

The record's punk theme had been partially abandoned to accommodate a bizarre range of covers—certain Guns N' Roses favourites were present and correct (the Sex Pistols via the obscure 'Black Leather' by guitarist Steve Jones; 'Attitude', the Misfits song that the band had regularly covered live on the tours following *Use Your Illusion I & II* with Duff on vocals), but this was no brace of familiar oldies given the once over. The selection process wasn't just

> "WHAT WE DO IS SUPPLY AN EVENING OF COMPLETE MAYHEM AND SOME COOL SONGS AND SWEAT. WE LIKE TO BRING SOME ELEMENT OF HAPHAZARD GOOD TIME..."
> *Slash*

Ronnie Wood pops up again (but it's Izzy's solo record he plays on).

made up of listing the top ten punk tunes of all time and playing them—it was further muddled by the band deciding that they wouldn't record a particular track unless the entire band (though this had clearly come to mean the trio of Axl, Slash and Duff) could agree on its seminal merits—so no David Bowie, despite Slash's desire to cut a Bowie tune "out of respect".

Instead we got a long-overdue Nazareth cover, some T-Rex, the Damned's 'New Rose', 'Ain't It Fun' by the Dead Boys and a song called 'Look At That Girl' originally recorded (and written, apparently) by

107

Right: Steven Adler—soon to settle out of court.

Charles Manson, the jailed mastermind behind seven cult murders that had shocked Los Angeles, and ultimately the world, in 1969. The track was tagged on after a gap at the end of the CD, and was unannounced on the sleeve. But if Guns N' Roses thought they'd slipped that past anyone, they were mistaken. They soon found themselves in the middle of a storm to equal the 'One In A Million' battles. Once again Guns N' Roses had hit a raw nerve and protests raged about the inappropriateness of the track. The band claimed to be unaware that Manson had written the song—and might, therefore, be eligible for royalties. However when they found that certain legal statutes prevented Manson from profiting, they decided to keep it on the record and donate royalties to Barteck Frrykowski, son of one of the victims of Manson's 'family'.

DARK EPITOME

"We naively thought there was a certain dark humour in Manson singing these love song lyrics at the time, but now I find the word 'humour' doesn't fit into the equation at all," explained Slash. "Especially when we

Left: Axl bathes in November rain.

Duff—from blond to brown

Duff gets rough—solo at London's Marquee club

think about the families of his victims and how this makes them feel. We didn't credit Manson on the album because we didn't want to draw any attention to him. We simply didn't anticipate everyone making such a big deal out of it. We especially don't want Manson to think we think he's bichin'—or anyone else to think it for that matter.

"There are no words to describe him as a human being. He's the epitome of what's wrong with human existence at this point and we don't want to glorify Manson in any way."

As with the 'One In A Million' debacle, Guns N' Roses had managed to shoot themselves in the foot. No amount of verbal squirming could detract from the fact that they'd indulged in a joke that had backfired badly.

USE YOUR IMAGINATION

At the time of writing, with Guns N' Roses reported to be already thinking in terms of a new album and anxious not to repeat the protracted delays of *Use Your Illusion I & II*, who knows what heroics and horrors the future holds?

One thing's for sure—no matter how jaded you

Next page: Axl and Stephanie— a wonderful couple

> **"WE'VE NEVER REHEARSED WITH AXL. SINCE WE STARTED OUT THAT'S NEVER HAPPENED BECAUSE WE'RE JUST TOO LOUD."**
> *Slash*

become with Guns N' Roses, they'll always bounce back when you least expect it and the headlines, once again, will be full of it. Anyone who loves committed, no-compromise rock'n'roll played loud and long, will wish them well and hope for the best.

But as Axl himself said: "Nothing ever really works right for this band. Slash once said that God didn't want this to happen, and sometimes I believe that."

Back to the club for Duff and his buddies

The Duffster's in limo heaven.

CHRONOLOGY

November 19, 1960—Birth of Matt Sorum

February 6, 1962—Birth of Axl Rose (as William Bailey)

April 8, 1967—Birth of Izzy Stradlin (as Jeff Isbell)

June 18, 1963—Birth of Dizzy Reed

February 5, 1964—Birth of Michael 'Duff' McKagan

July 23, 1965—Birth of Saul 'Slash' Hudson

January 22, 1965—Birth of Steven Adler

1984/85—Guns N' Roses evolve from two local Los Angeles bands, Hollywood Rose and LA Guns. **June 1985**—Slash and Steven Adler of Road Crew join in time for Guns N' Roses brief 'Hell Tour'—first gigs by the 'classic' line-up

August 1986—Guns N' Roses sign to Geffen Records

December 1986—Guns N' Roses release their *Live ?!*@ Like A Suicide* EP, in a limited edition of 10,000 vinyl copies, on Uzi Suicide Records (a pseudo-independent imprint created by Geffen for the band)

June, 1987—The band fly to London for their European debut, three (non-consecutive) nights at the Marquee club

August 1987—*Appetite For Destruction* released

November 1987—Guns N' Roses return to the UK for a five-date headlining tour

August 1988—Third European visit, to play Monsters Of Rock at Castle Donington in the UK. Tragically, two fans are killed in the crush in front of the stage

December 1988—*Guns N' Roses Lies—The Sex, The Drugs, The Violence, The Shocking Truth* is released with four new acoustic tracks plus the four tracks from *Live ?!*@ Like A Suicide*

October 1989—The band play four packed gigs with the Rolling Stones at the Los Angeles Colliseum

April 1990—The band play the Farm Aid concert and recruit Dizzy Reed, the first 'new' member of Guns N' Roses, to play keyboards

July 1990—Steven Adler is fired

August 1990—Ex-Cult drummer Matt Sorum is recruited

January 1991—New line-up debuts in front of 140,000 fans at the Rock In Rio II festival in Brazil

May 1991—Guns N' Roses begin their mammoth world tour, dubbed 'Get In The Ring', with 'live rehearsals' at clubs in San Francisco, Los Angeles and New York

July 1991—Guns N' Roses find themselves in the middle of a riot at the Riverport Arts Centre in St Louis and a warrant is issued for Axl's arrest for inciting it

Roses set in Montreal, Canada. The same night, Metallica's James Hetfield is badly burned by on-stage pyrotechnics

November 1992—Guns N' Roses tour South America

December 1992—Guns N' Roses release two concert videos: *Use Your Illusion World Tour* and *Live In Tokyo Volumes I & II*

January 1993—Pacific tour covers Australia, New Zealand and Japan

February 1993—American touring continues, with a slimmed-down line-up and a new title 'Skin And Bones'

May 1993—Izzy Stradlin briefly rejoins the band for European dates including gigs in the UK, Greece and Israel

July 1993—The world touring finally ends with a return to Brazil

September 1993—The band settle their legal differences with Steven Adler, with a $2.5 (£1.7) million out-of-court payment

October 1993—Duff McKagan releases *Believe In Me*, a solo album recorded during the band's world tour

November 1993—The punk EP is finally released as a full-length album of varied cover-versions, called *The Spaghetti Incident?*

August 1991—The band play European stadium gigs for a month

September 1991—The band finally release *Use Your Illusion Volumes I & II*. Izzy Stradlin is rumoured to have quit the band only days later

October 1991—Steven Adler files legal proceedings against Guns N' Roses

November 1991—Izzy's departure made official

April 6, 1992—Guns N' Roses appear at the Freddie Mercury Tribute Concert For AIDS Awareness

May 1992—Slash and Metallica's Lars Ulrich announce a joint summer tour of America, before Guns N' Roses play another series of European dates

July 1992—Guns N' Roses and Metallica begin their 25-date US tour

August 1992—A riot follows a disrupted Guns N'

DISCOGRAPHY

Released Albums

Albums	Title	Label	CD
1986	Live ?!*@ Like A Suicide	Uzi Suicide Records	VSR-001
Aug 1987	Appetite For Destruction	Geffen	GEFD 24148
Dec 1988	Guns N' Roses Lies—The Sex, The Drugs, The Violence, The Shocking Truth	Geffen	GEFD 24198
Sep 1991	Use Your Illusion I	Geffen	GEFD 24415
Sep 1991	Use Your Illusion II	Geffen	GEFD 24420
Nov 1993	The Spaghetti Incident?	Geffen	GED 24617

Singles

Oct 1988	Welcome To The Jungle (re-release)	Geffen	GEF 47CD
Mar 1989	Paradise City	Geffen	GEF 50CD
May 1989	Sweet Child O' Mine (re-release)	Geffen	GEF 55CD
Jun 1989	Patience	Geffen	GEF 56CD
Aug 1989	Night Train	Geffen	GEF 60CD
Jul 1991	You Could Be Mine	Geffen	GFSTD 6
Aug 1991	Don't Cry	Geffen	GFSTD 9
Dec 1991	Live And Let Die	Geffen	GFSTD 17
Feb 1992	November Rain	Geffen	GFSTD 18
May 1992	Knockin' On Heaven's Door	Geffen	GFSTD 21
Nov 1992	Yesterdays	Geffen	GFSTD 27
May 1993	The Civil War EP	Geffen	GEFSTD 43

Solo Albums

Izzy Stradlin And The Ju Ju Hounds

Oct 1992	Izzy Stradlin And The Ju Ju Hounds	Geffen	GED 24490

Duff McKagan

1993	Believe In Me	Geffen	GED 24605

INDEX

PICTURE ACKNOWLEDGMENTS

Photographs preproduced by kind
permisson of **London Features
International**; **Pictorial Press**/ Todd
Kaplan,/Bob Leafe,/Jeffrey Mayer,/Brian
Rasic,/Lee Windward; **Redferns**/Mick
Hutson,/Ebet Roberts; **Retna
Pictures**/Steve Granitz,/Gene
Krikland,/Eddie Mallut,/Tony
Mottram,/Neal Preston,/Aaron
Rappaport,/Ian Tilton,/Timothy White;
Rex Features/Action Press,/Fotos
International,/I.B.L.,/L.G.I.,/Vivienne
Ventura.
Front cover picture: London Features
International